Cricket Betting And The Fake ICC World Cup 2023

Atul Kumar

DIAMOND BOOKS

www.diamondbook.in

Publisher : **Diamond Pocket Books (P) Ltd.**
X-30, Okhla Industrial Area, Phase-II
New Delhi-110020
Phone : 011-40712200
E-mail : sales@dpb.in
Website : www.dpb.in
Edition : 2024
Printed by : Repro (India)

Cricket Betting And The Fake ICC World Cup 2023
Author : *Atul Kumar*

To

Diamond Books

the rare publisher who doesn't hesitate
to publish the Truth.

Preface

By the time I completed my recent book *'IPL-2023 Mount Everest of Crime and Corruption'*, the ICC World Cup had already started in India. In that book, I had penned down the following:

'Let us think about another fundamental thing. How and on what basis the betting odds are opened and continuously changed for match result, session, or other fancy bets? Is there any mathematical/scientific formula? Answer is a big No. Who controls the odds, on what authority, and/or on what basis? It remains a matter of record that all or almost all the bookies and regular betting websites follow the same odds worldwide.

After opening arbitrarily, the odds for session and many other fancy bets may appear to be changing logically; but can there be and is there any logic for how the odds suddenly change for match result with the progress of a match (the opening odds again being arbitrary)? When will the odds change how much, especially on fall of a wicket or on a boundary or a flurry of boundary hits? How is that decided?

There are concrete mentions in my previous books/writings of how the odds changed in matches to suit the whims of the mafia, defying logic. Those who bet and keenly follow the odds can come across this phenomenon, match after match.

If one were to apply mind to management (that mostly is manipulation) **of the odds alone, one would understand that**

the betting and rigging had to go together. There is a clear record of this fact also that the odds in cricket were managed by the mafia well knowing what was going to happen in a match. That has been in full knowledge of the media and the judicial commissions appointed on the subject of fixing in cricket, since almost a decade. **But unfortunately, to ignore it has suited all.** This has amply been brought out earlier by me, also to the knowledge of the Supreme Court of India. Alas! the world has been acting blind to this hard and very valuable fact also!'

I had also mentioned that the majority of cricket lovers didn't know much about betting. So, fresh from completing draft of the last book, I got an idea. To try to make the masses aware about the prevalent large-scale betting. To give sufficient examples through the Cricket World Cup 2023 to the ordinary cricket fans so that they could comprehend ever better how the Cricket they were crazy about was totally fake - a puppet show being performed for astronomical financial gains to the cricket betting mafia. How fake and false has been the existence of the world with regards to Cricket, and hence otherwise also, at least for last some decades! I hope that this book will serve that purpose.

In the light of my previous books, press conferences, published interviews, news items, detailed Writ Petition (PIL) in the Supreme Court of India, and many other writings on the subject including in the social media, especially the page https://www.facebook.com/BettorsBeware/, **this book does amount to reinventing the wheel**. But it appears that the world, ignorant still, does need it!

–Atul Kumar
November, 2023

Contents

Cricket Betting and CWC 2023

There are tens or hundreds of millions of cricket bettors in the world. Still, the vast majority of a few billion cricket fans don't bet and have only very superficial knowledge about cricket betting.

Most of us know that for most of the matches anywhere in any format, there are betting odds for win or loss of a team. For example, starting odds for a team to win may be 1.38 - 1.39 (meaning that one betting for that team to win will get additional 38 paisa or 0.38 dollars for every one rupee or dollar wagered respectively, and the one betting for the opposite team to win will get additional 1/.39 = 2.56 rupees or dollars for every one rupee or dollar wagered).

We don't know how these odds are decided or arrived upon, we have only our beliefs in this regard. Who does it and on what authority? But these odds are centrally controlled worldwide and the same odds are used by all the bookies - hundreds and thousands of them, and all the betting websites – scores and hundreds of those, may be with some negligible variation here or there. **Addicted to betting, and lured by the prospects of making easy money, the millions and millions of bettors globally continue to place bets nevertheless (mostly to lose) worth tens of billions of dollars daily, remaining in the dark all the time about the origin and control of the bets etc.**

But something very important and valuable is officially known. **One**, Times of India news report dated 27/7/2013 and titled *'IPL betting rates set by Dawood, says chargesheet'* had this to tell, '....Delhi Police's chargesheet, likely to be filed next week, is expected to explain how Dawood was not above pulling a fast one even on bookies who trusted D-company's "tip offs", pointing to the treacherous world of illegal betting controlled by the don.

"Small and middle level bookies trusted the winning team information announced by D-company as this mostly turns out to be true. But sometimes, the information was faked. A wrong winning team would be named. So, while some bookies knew where to place money, others who took the D-company information at face value lost. Both ways, D company benefitted," said a senior police officer....'

Two, following is in the Mudgal Committee report as brought out in the book *'Fixed!: Cash and Corruption in Cricket'* (a rare valuable book on Cricket) by the awarded veteran journalist Shantanu Guha ray: '...Chutani would routinely convey opening rates to key bookies in India, Pakistan, Singapore, and Kuala Lumpur. He was sure about what would happen in a match and rates were fixed accordingly....' Javed Chutani has been mentioned as one of very few in the inner circle of Dawood Ibrahim, in direct touch with him.

A little application of mind to the above two alone should be enough to make anyone endowed with some commonsense realise that the cricket betting odds were decided by the betting mafia controlled by Dawood Ibrahim those days, with full prior knowledge as to what would happen in a match, and not on any other basis; various beliefs of the myriad people notwithstanding. **Irrespective of anything else, this alone tells us that the betting odds and their movement didn't**

depend upon how the play was progressing, but it was the other way round. Play in the grounds followed the betting odds and how those were supposed to move. The opening odds for various matches in the CWC 2023 (as enumerated in the next chapter), and the movements in those odds amply demonstrated this.

Consequently, it does mean that all the matches were institutionally fixed and scripted from start to finish. All the talk of spot fixing here or there, of random bookies luring random players, of complaints by some players at times of approach by shadowy characters etc. was all hogwash, broadly created to camouflage the reality and to keep the billions in the world constantly fooled. So was the action against some players now and then; that could also be for the reasons that those players tried to play smart with the authorities to earn some extra bucks. Any talk about Cricket notwithstanding, the institutional scripting had to be in place all the time for the very survival of the big betting industry, and for exponential gains to it. **It's so simple.**

The betting odds for a match don't remain static, but continue to move up or down with the progress of a match. For example, in Australia vs Afghanistan match on the 7th November, 2023, the starting odds before toss were 1.14 -1.15 in favour of Australia, after toss the same were 1.18 -1.19. The odds went on varying/moving throughout such that when Australia were 91/7 while chasing, the odds were around 1.00 – 1.01 in f/o Afghanistan. These odds continued to increase for Afghanistan win with the 8th wicket partnership in progress till Australia finally won. We can see another example also so that this aspect becomes clearer to the readers.

In the Netherland vs England match played the next day on the 8th November, the odds were 1.14 -1.15 in favour of England before the toss. After that the odds moved downwards only in f/o England till England won the one-sided contest. At innings break, the odds were 1.05 -1.06 (much less than the starting odds) in f/o England, even though England had scored about 30 runs less than the bookies' expectation. We shall see this aspect in some detail later on to understand its significance, if not clear to some readers now.

As already mentioned, the starting odds and movement of odds for many matches in this World Cup quite conspicuously confirmed what we have already inferred and known above from the hard facts on record. That those deciding on and controlling the odds and their movement well knew in advance what was going to happen in the matches, like the puppeteers know as to what will happen next in a puppet show; while the billions across the globe watched the matches with a sense of suspense and with bated breath.

Nothing gives away the whole façade of Cricket better than **Session Betting.** The betting in cricket doesn't take place for which team will win alone. Many a time or in many matches, betting takes place on the runs to be scored in various sessions, a session consisting of given number of overs. It is popularly known as *session betting*. In this World Cup, the session betting was mostly available for every 5 overs in the first innings, and at least for the first 5 and 10 overs in the second innings. In session betting, probably maximum betting takes place for the innings score in the first innings. Many times, betting for the innings score is available in the second innings also, especially when the chasing team falls well behind the target. That happened often in this World Cup.

Then, there are innumerable fancy bets, i.e., bets for sundry possibilities in the course of a match, including bets placed for runs scored of every ball at times, performances by individual players, fall of wickets etc. One can have an idea of what type of bets are available from the following screen shots of a betting website during semifinal between India and New Zealand at a random point of time:

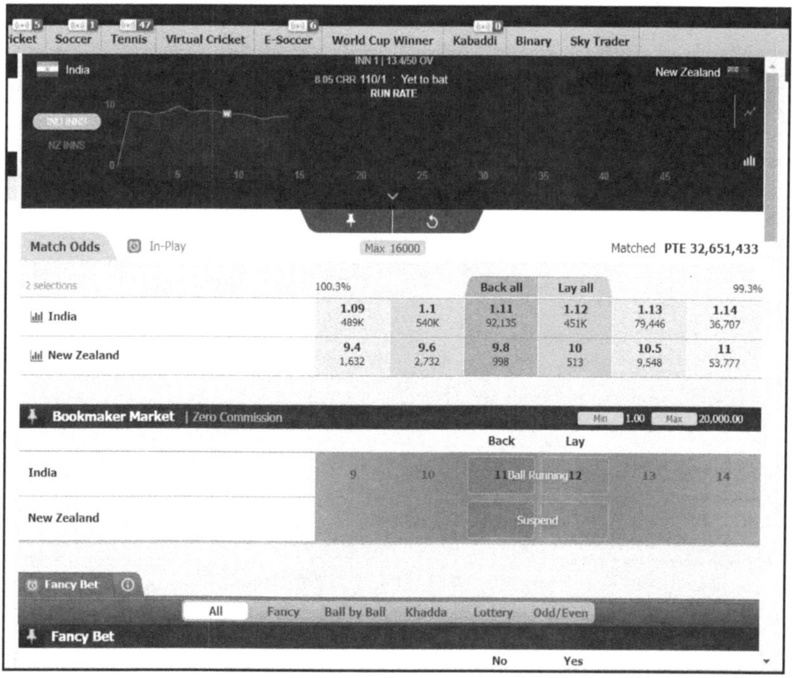
Soccer
Tennis
Virtual Cricket
E-Soccer
World Cup Winner
Kabaddi
Binary
Sky Trader
India
INN 1 | 13.4/50 OV
8.05 CRR 110/1 : Yet to bat
RUN RATE
New Zealand
Match Odds
In-Play
Max 16000
Matched PTE 32,651,433
2 selections
100.3%
Back all
Lay all
99.3%
India
1.09 489K
1.1 540K
1.11 92,135
1.12 451K
1.13 79,446
1.14 36,707
New Zealand
9.4 1,632
9.6 2,732
9.8 998
10 513
10.5 9,548
11 53,777
Bookmaker Market
| Zero Commission
Min 1.00
Max 20,000.00
Back
Lay
India
9
10
11
Ball Running
12
13
14
New Zealand
Suspend
Fancy Bet
All
Fancy
Ball by Ball
Khadda
Lottery
Odd/Even
Fancy Bet
No
Yes

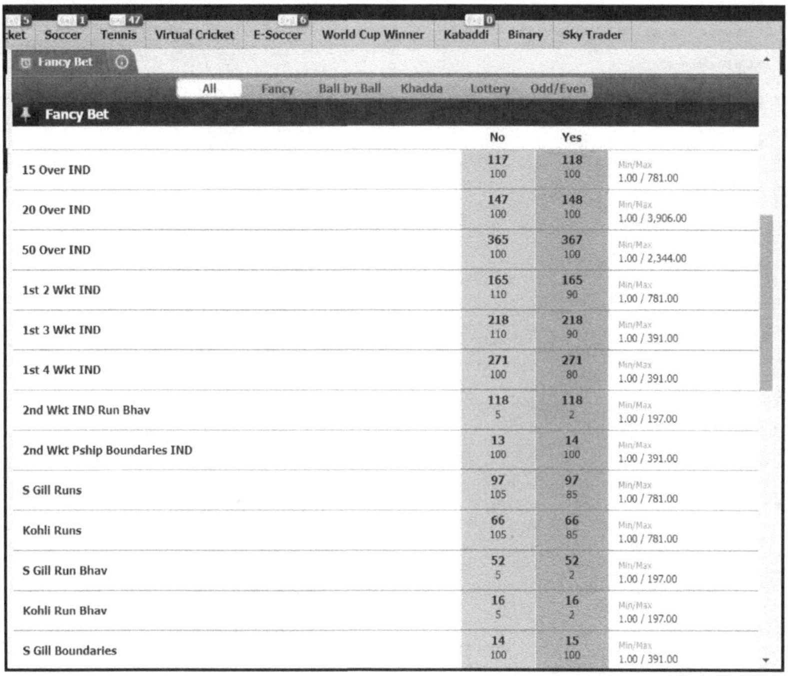

ket | Soccer | Tennis | Virtual Cricket | E-Soccer | World Cup Winner | Kabaddi | Binary | Sky Trader

Fancy Bet

All | Fancy | Ball by Ball | Khadda | Lottery | Odd/Even

Fancy Bet

	No	Yes	
15 Over IND	117 100	118 100	Min/Max 1.00 / 781.00
20 Over IND	147 100	148 100	Min/Max 1.00 / 3,906.00
50 Over IND	365 100	367 100	Min/Max 1.00 / 2,344.00
1st 2 Wkt IND	165 110	165 90	Min/Max 1.00 / 781.00
1st 3 Wkt IND	218 110	218 90	Min/Max 1.00 / 391.00
1st 4 Wkt IND	271 100	271 80	Min/Max 1.00 / 391.00
2nd Wkt IND Run Bhav	118 5	118 2	Min/Max 1.00 / 197.00
2nd Wkt Pship Boundaries IND	13 100	14 100	Min/Max 1.00 / 391.00
S Gill Runs	97 105	97 85	Min/Max 1.00 / 781.00
Kohli Runs	66 105	66 85	Min/Max 1.00 / 781.00
S Gill Run Bhav	52 5	52 2	Min/Max 1.00 / 197.00
Kohli Run Bhav	16 5	16 2	Min/Max 1.00 / 197.00
S Gill Boundaries	14 100	15 100	Min/Max 1.00 / 391.00

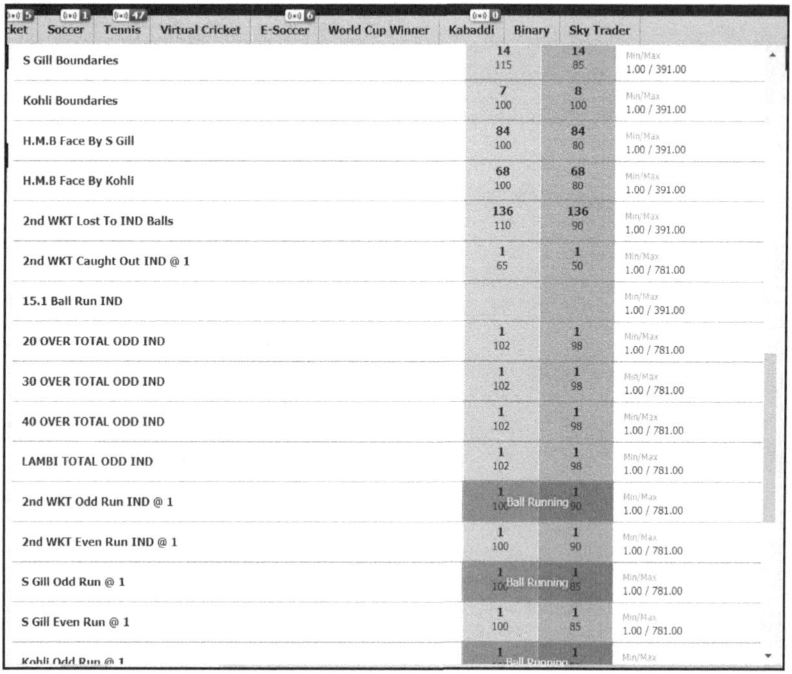

ket | Soccer | Tennis | Virtual Cricket | E-Soccer | World Cup Winner | Kabaddi | Binary | Sky Trader

Market	No	Yes	Min/Max
S Gill Boundaries	14 115	14 85	1.00 / 391.00
Kohli Boundaries	7 100	8 100	1.00 / 391.00
H.M.B Face By S Gill	84 100	84 80	1.00 / 391.00
H.M.B Face By Kohli	68 100	68 80	1.00 / 391.00
2nd WKT Lost To IND Balls	136 110	136 90	1.00 / 391.00
2nd WKT Caught Out IND @ 1	1 65	1 50	1.00 / 781.00
15.1 Ball Run IND			1.00 / 391.00
20 OVER TOTAL ODD IND	1 102	1 98	1.00 / 781.00
30 OVER TOTAL ODD IND	1 102	1 98	1.00 / 781.00
40 OVER TOTAL ODD IND	1 102	1 98	1.00 / 781.00
LAMBI TOTAL ODD IND	1 102	1 98	1.00 / 781.00
2nd WKT Odd Run IND @ 1	1 100 Ball Running	1 90	1.00 / 781.00
2nd WKT Even Run IND @ 1	1 100	1 90	1.00 / 781.00
S Gill Odd Run @ 1	1 100 Ball Running	1 85	1.00 / 781.00
S Gill Even Run @ 1	1 100	1 85	1.00 / 781.00
Kohli Odd Run @ 1	1	1	

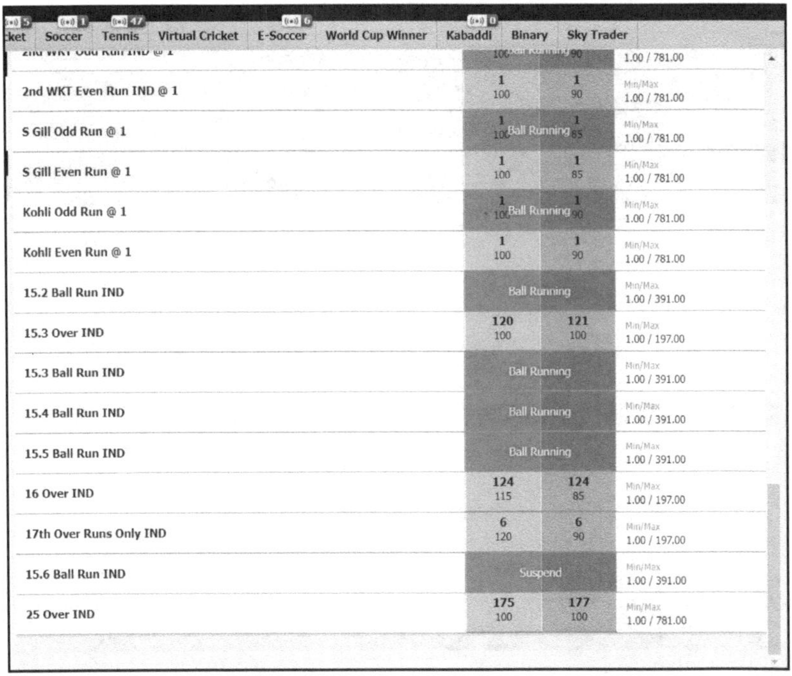

ket | Soccer | Tennis | Virtual Cricket | E-Soccer | World Cup Winner | Kabaddi | Binary | Sky Trader

Market	Back	Lay	Min/Max
2nd WKT Odd Run IND @ 1	100	90	1.00 / 781.00
2nd WKT Even Run IND @ 1	1 100	1 90	Min/Max 1.00 / 781.00
S Gill Odd Run @ 1	1 100 Ball Running	1 85	Min/Max 1.00 / 781.00
S Gill Even Run @ 1	1 100	1 85	Min/Max 1.00 / 781.00
Kohli Odd Run @ 1	1 100 Ball Running	1 90	Min/Max 1.00 / 781.00
Kohli Even Run @ 1	1 100	1 90	Min/Max 1.00 / 781.00
15.2 Ball Run IND	Ball Running		Min/Max 1.00 / 391.00
15.3 Over IND	120 100	121 100	Min/Max 1.00 / 197.00
15.3 Ball Run IND	Ball Running		Min/Max 1.00 / 391.00
15.4 Ball Run IND	Ball Running		Min/Max 1.00 / 391.00
15.5 Ball Run IND	Ball Running		Min/Max 1.00 / 391.00
16 Over IND	124 115	124 85	Min/Max 1.00 / 197.00
17th Over Runs Only IND	6 120	6 90	Min/Max 1.00 / 197.00
15.6 Ball Run IND	Suspend		Min/Max 1.00 / 391.00
25 Over IND	175 100	177 100	Min/Max 1.00 / 781.00

The following bets were available after the Indian innings or in the New Zealand innings:

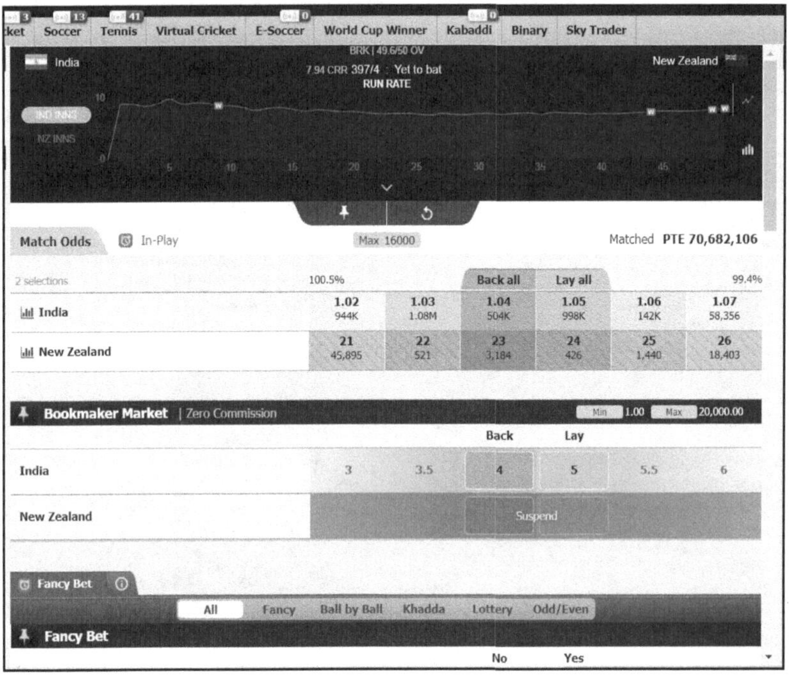
Soccer
Tennis
Virtual Cricket
E-Soccer
World Cup Winner
Kabaddi
Binary
Sky Trader
India
New Zealand
7.94 CRR 397/4 : Yet to bat
RUN RATE
Match Odds
In-Play
Max 16000
Matched PTE 70,682,106
Back all
Lay all
India 1.02 1.03 1.04 1.05 1.06 1.07
New Zealand 21 22 23 24 25 26
Bookmaker Market | Zero Commission
Back
Lay
India 3 3.5 4 5 5.5 6
New Zealand
Suspend
Fancy Bet
All Fancy Ball by Ball Khadda Lottery Odd/Even
Fancy Bet
No Yes

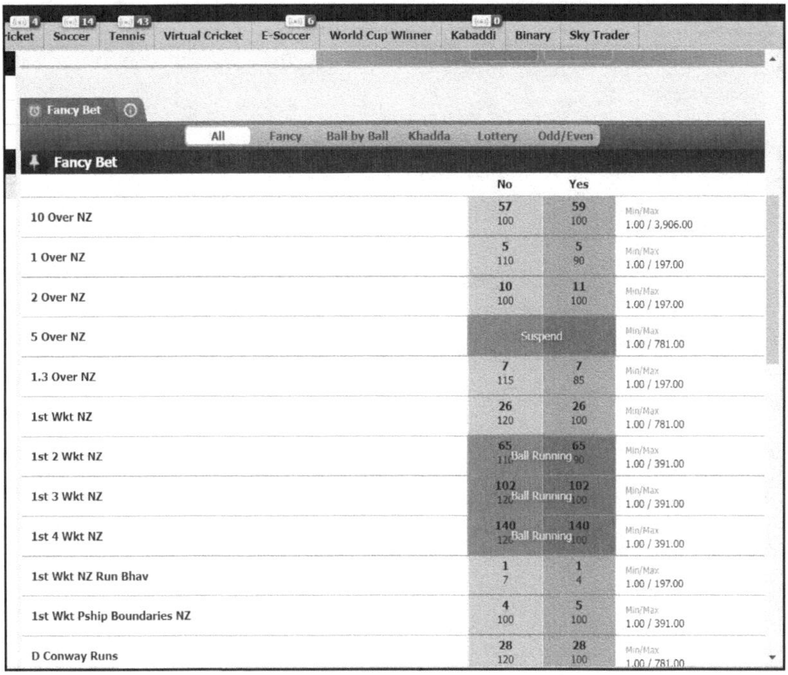
Soccer
Tennis
Virtual Cricket
E-Soccer
World Cup Winner
Kabaddi
Binary
Sky Trader
Fancy Bet
All
Fancy
Ball by Ball
Khadda
Lottery
Odd/Even
Fancy Bet
No
Yes
10 Over NZ
57 100
59 100
Min/Max 1.00 / 3,906.00
1 Over NZ
5 110
5 90
Min/Max 1.00 / 197.00
2 Over NZ
10 100
11 100
Min/Max 1.00 / 197.00
5 Over NZ
Suspend
Min/Max 1.00 / 781.00
1.3 Over NZ
7 115
7 85
Min/Max 1.00 / 197.00
1st Wkt NZ
26 120
26 100
Min/Max 1.00 / 781.00
1st 2 Wkt NZ
Ball Running
Min/Max 1.00 / 391.00
1st 3 Wkt NZ
Ball Running
Min/Max 1.00 / 391.00
1st 4 Wkt NZ
Ball Running
Min/Max 1.00 / 391.00
1st Wkt NZ Run Bhav
1 7
1 4
Min/Max 1.00 / 197.00
1st Wkt Pship Boundaries NZ
4 100
5 100
Min/Max 1.00 / 391.00
D Conway Runs
28 120
28 100
Min/Max

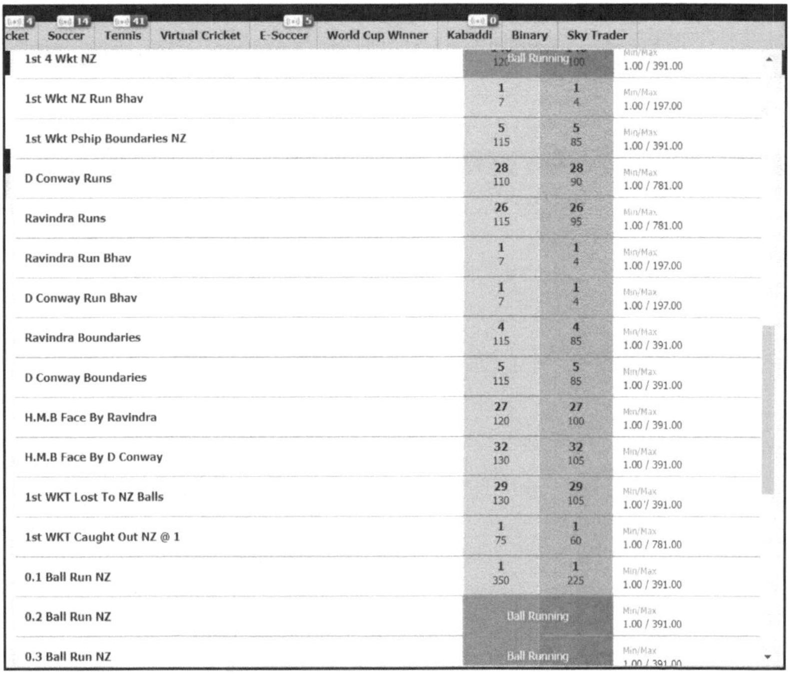

cket | Soccer | Tennis | Virtual Cricket | E-Soccer | World Cup Winner | Kabaddi | Binary | Sky Trader

Market			Min/Max
1st 4 Wkt NZ	120 Ball Running	100	1.00 / 391.00
1st Wkt NZ Run Bhav	1 7	1 4	1.00 / 197.00
1st Wkt Pship Boundaries NZ	5 115	5 85	1.00 / 391.00
D Conway Runs	28 110	28 90	1.00 / 781.00
Ravindra Runs	26 115	26 95	1.00 / 781.00
Ravindra Run Bhav	1 7	1 4	1.00 / 197.00
D Conway Run Bhav	1 7	1 4	1.00 / 197.00
Ravindra Boundaries	4 115	4 85	1.00 / 391.00
D Conway Boundaries	5 115	5 85	1.00 / 391.00
H.M.B Face By Ravindra	27 120	27 100	1.00 / 391.00
H.M.B Face By D Conway	32 130	32 105	1.00 / 391.00
1st WKT Lost To NZ Balls	29 130	29 105	1.00 / 391.00
1st WKT Caught Out NZ @ 1	1 75	1 60	1.00 / 781.00
0.1 Ball Run NZ	1 350	1 225	1.00 / 391.00
0.2 Ball Run NZ	Ball Running		1.00 / 391.00
0.3 Ball Run NZ	Ball Running		1.00 / 391.00

cket 4	Soccer 14	Tennis 41	Virtual Cricket	E-Soccer 5	World Cup Winner	Kabaddi 0	Binary	Sky Trader

Market			Min/Max
0.2 Ball Run NZ	Ball Running		1.00 / 391.00
0.3 Ball Run NZ	Ball Running		1.00 / 391.00
0.4 Ball Run NZ	Ball Running		1.00 / 391.00
0.5 Ball Run NZ	Ball Running		1.00 / 391.00
0.6 Ball Run NZ	Suspend		1.00 / 391.00
10 OVER TOTAL ODD NZ	1 102	1 98	1.00 / 781.00
20 OVER TOTAL ODD NZ	1 102	1 98	1.00 / 781.00
30 OVER TOTAL ODD NZ	1 102	1 98	1.00 / 781.00
40 OVER TOTAL ODD NZ	1 102	1 98	1.00 / 781.00
1st WKT Odd Run NZ @ 1	Ball Running		1.00 / 781.00
1st WKT Even Run NZ @ 1	1 100	1 90	1.00 / 781.00
D Conway Odd Run @ 1	1 100 Ball Running	1 90	1.00 / 781.00
D Conway Even Run @ 1	1 100	1 85	1.00 / 781.00
Ravindra Odd Run @ 1	1 100 Ball Running	1 90	1.00 / 781.00
Ravindra Even Run @ 1	1 100	1 85	1.00 / 781.00

The odds in the purple box on the left for various bets are the odds to lay against that bet and in the blue box on the right are the odds for backing the bet. For example, at that point of time, one could bet against New Zealand scoring 57 runs or more in the first 10 overs, or could bet for New Zealand scoring 59 or more runs in those 10 overs. Like for match result, these odds also are dynamic and change with the progress of the match for most of the bets. The list of various bets available as above is not exhaustive, it is only suggestive. Many more bets with many more permutations and combinations can be/are available.

The purpose of above is only to give the readers an idea of the various fancy bets available to the bettors, in addition to the bets for match result. Those not conversant with betting may not bother much about how these bets are placed or how these are decided. It should suffice for them to know what all bets are available, one or another bet being decided at almost every ball. Every ball does affect the outcome of/ movement in many ongoing bets, till a match is over.

Session betting also can be termed as a fancy bet, though even more popular than the match result at times. Bracket betting is another variation of session betting, not much in vogue in India and hardly available on the betting sites functional in India. **One must understand what session betting is all about.**

Session betting and bracket betting mean that you are being offered to bet on whether so many runs will be scored or not in so many overs. Offer to bet on runs to be scored in a particular ball or in a particular over should fall in the category of other fancy bets, and not session betting. From session, I understand a set of overs. https://betindia.in/betting-academy/how-to-bet-on-cricket/session-in-cricket-betting/ gives another overview of session betting by someone else, apparently from the perspective of the betting industry. While on the subject of session betting, one should also peruse https://www.espncricinfo.com/story/rashid-latif-how-cricket-matches-are-scripted-468255. The infamous Sreesanth episode of IPL 6 in 2013 also related to session betting.

When people tend to dismiss session fixing as some inconsequential spot fixing, they talk through their hat. There can't be anything like stand-alone session fixing. Almost every time, any fixed session will have a bearing on the match result (except probably in manipulation of innings score by a chasing team in some cases after it hardly had any chance of winning). Fixing of even a small session necessarily involves participation of many players and umpires etc. It won't make sense to any sane mind that all those involved play fixed cricket sometime and start playing competitively some other time in the same match. That has been explained in more detail in the chapter *'It's elementary, My dear Watson!'* in my last book **'IPL-2023 Mount Everest of Crime and Corruption'.** Earlier it was explained 10 years ago in the chapter *'Large Scale Fixing Gets Established but All look the Other Way'* in my book 'Bettors Beware' (subsequently republished under the title 'All Cricket Matches are Fixed'), based on the Sreesanth episode.

If one understood session betting, had some experience of it, and had the slightest common sense, in no time it would have dawned on one that the prevalence of session betting continuously for decades itself was sufficient to announce ball-by-ball or almost ball-by-ball scripting and fixing of cricket matches, irrespective of or independent of anything else. The session betting just couldn't exist without continuous rigging in the matches. **Therefore, to be truthful, to analyze or discuss anything else for deliberating on the extent of fixing in Cricket is simply redundant.**

How do bookies estimate the runs to be scored in an innings, how do they know in advance whether it will be high score or low score? Is it not often that you discover that the bookies knew better than what the commentators or the experts told you? How do they estimate the runs to be scored in a set of overs? How do they know when the batsmen will go into a shell or when they will start scoring briskly? How can anyone take the risk of offering bets on session and going pauper (since scoring could be much different from what the bookies thought)? Answer to all above is rather obvious and simple. Those controlling the session bets know in advance how scoring will go on or proceed in a match. That would mean that they have to be knowing the outcome of every or almost every ball beforehand.

As the odds for match result go on changing, similarly the session score being offered by the bookies also goes on changing. One would find that often the scoring in a session is such that the end session score either exceeds all or almost all the sessions (the popular term for 'session score') offered by the bookies or is less than all or almost all the offers. One can see that it happened so in many sessions in the ICC men's CWC (Cricket World Cup) 2023. Sessions have to be kept that way quite frequently. Why?. Because otherwise punters can repeatedly place bets to make use of the windows they will get and thus win huge amounts minimizing their risk or having no risk.

Let us try to understand this from an example. Suppose the session offer varied between 240/242 and 281/283 throughout a 50 over innings, and the end score was 257. A punter placing bets for 247 and against 265 during the innings would have won both his bets with no risk of losing if the bets were for equal amounts. Sometimes you can definitely win in this fashion in session betting, but such a scenario can't be allowed quite often by those running the show. If so, the punters will be at tremendous advantage vis-à-vis the bookies/betting sites in session betting. **And such a scenario would present itself many times in almost all the sessions if natural cricket was played! That's why session betting and natural cricket just can't go together.**

As researched and recorded in my earlier books, about 2/3 of all the sessions were so manipulated that punters got no advantage of the windows mentioned above, **even though the probability of so happening was one in trillions for natural competitive cricket**. That actual percentage could change temporarily (from broad percentage of 65 plus), but it is a compulsion for the puppeteers to keep the percentage high in the longer run, as long as the betting on sessions continues.

We shall see how the odds, sessions, and their movement in the CWC 2023 was nothing but a manifestation of all that we have discussed above, confirming a thoroughly scripted World Cup.

The readers must bear in mind that the cricket betting including the session betting, the odds, and their movement in the World Cup was a hard fact, something totally objective; while the viewers' impressions, their beliefs, the commentators' and experts' comments and opinions, pitch reports, the social media posts etc. were all subjective things. First and foremost, we must see what we learn objectively or scientifically; forgetting all the subjectivity that has been conditioning our minds since our birth. Shastris, Gavaskars, Pontings, Kohlis, Dhonis, Tendulkars, Kapil Devs, Dhonis et-al who have been conditioning our minds for ages, all belong to the same school that controls the thoroughly corrupt Cricket.

One more thing. When those not knowing much about betting or session betting tend to be all knowledgeable about cricket matches or the subject of fixing in cricket, **that's like**

someone feeling that he/she knows all about an ocean after having seen only a pond.

10 years ago, session betting was the basis for me to prove mathematically and hence scientifically, **beyond any ifs and buts**, that the Cricket matches that were betted upon and we saw were all fixed and scripted ball-by-ball or almost so. **Applying the principles detailed (in the book *'Bettors Beware'*), one can know for sure from the score books alone whether a match was fixed, without needing to view a single ball of the match.** The contents of the book remain unchallenged by anyone, even by the all-powerful ICC, for 10 long years. On the other hand, the same lie vindicated by two reputed veterans, years and miles apart, who bothered to examine.

❐

Betting Odds and Sessions during CWC 2023

The following screenshots from some app give a record of starting odds or almost starting odds (after first ball) for all the matches in the CWC 2023. On the left are scores after the ball (e.g., 0.2 means 0.2 overs or 2 balls in the first over) indicated alongside. On the right, the bottom line gives session on offer and the line above shows the odds for the match result at that point of time.

The figures in blue on the left mean the offer for laying, and in red on the right give the offer for backing. For example, the first screen shot is for the first match between England and New Zealand. It shows that after the first ball, score of England was 0/0. Then the 10 over session score on offer by the bookies was 56-57; and the odds in f/o England were 1.58-1.59. After the second ball, score of England was 6/0. Then the 10 over session score on offer by the bookies changed to 62-63; and the odds in f/o England to 1.49-1.50. So on.

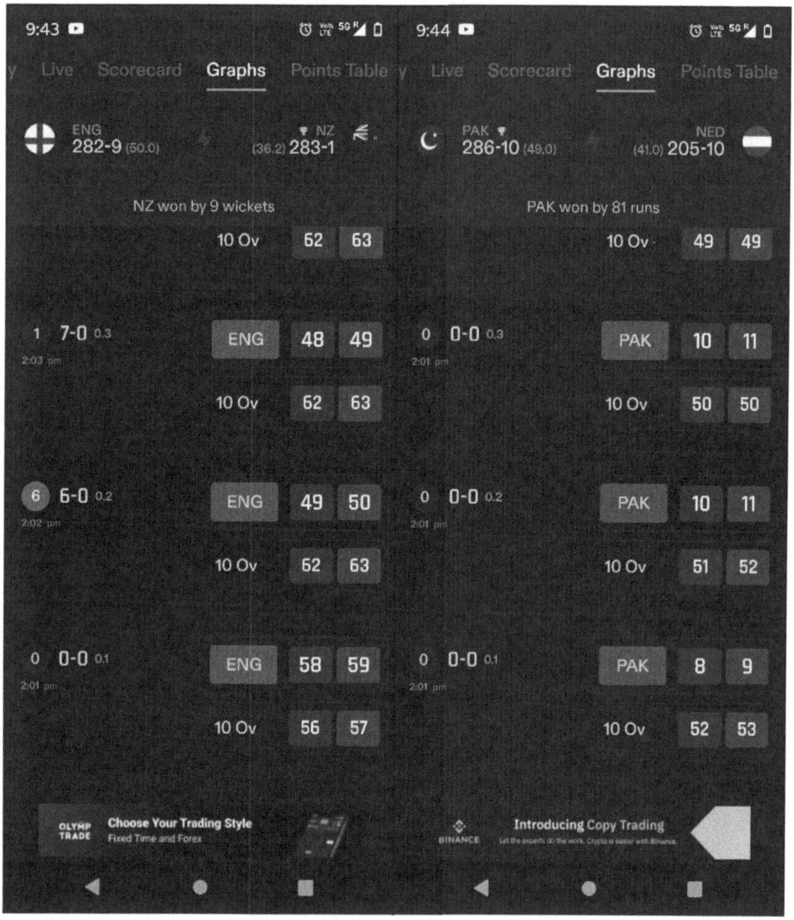
9:43
Live
Scorecard
Graphs
Points Table
ENG
282-9 (50.0)
NZ
(36.2) 283-1
NZ won by 9 wickets
10 Ov 62 63
1 7-0 0.3
2:03 pm
ENG 48 49
10 Ov 62 63
6 6-0 0.2
2:02 pm
ENG 49 50
10 Ov 62 63
0 0-0 0.1
2:01 pm
ENG 58 59
10 Ov 56 57
OLYMP TRADE
Choose Your Trading Style
Fixed Time and Forex
9:44
Live
Scorecard
Graphs
Points Table
PAK
286-10 (49.0)
NED
(41.0) 205-10
PAK won by 81 runs
10 Ov 49 49
0 0-0 0.3
2:01 pm
PAK 10 11
10 Ov 50 50
0 0-0 0.2
2:01 pm
PAK 10 11
10 Ov 51 52
0 0-0 0.1
2:01 pm
PAK 8 9
10 Ov 52 53
BINANCE
Introducing Copy Trading

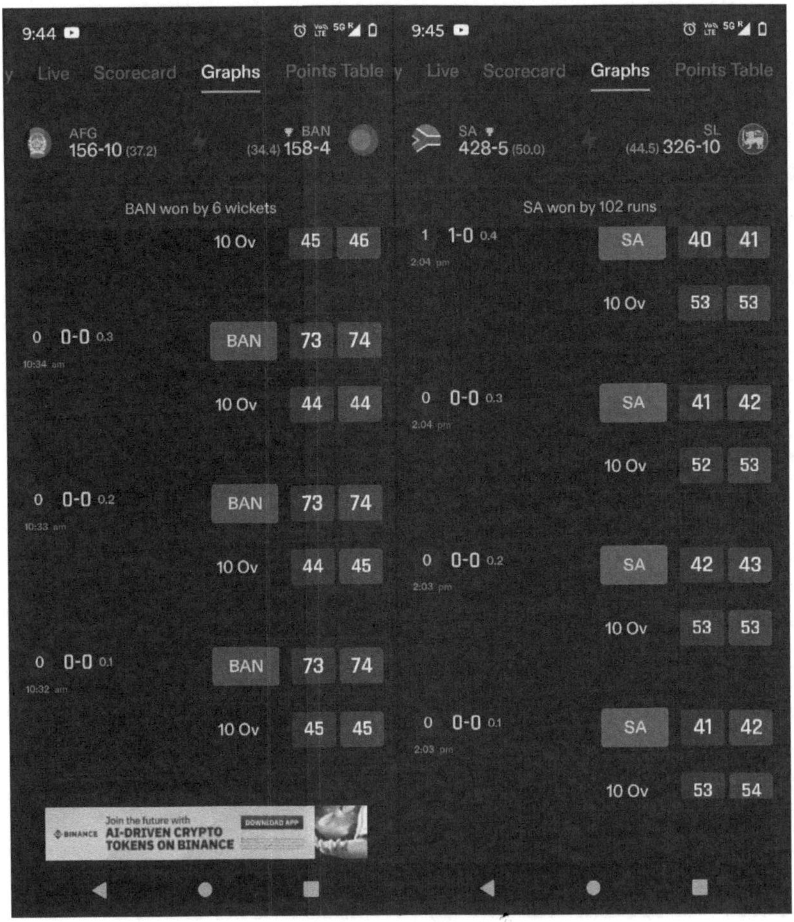
9:44
Live Scorecard Graphs Points Table
AFG
156-10 (37.2)
BAN
(34.4) 158-4
BAN won by 6 wickets
10 Ov 45 46
0 0-0 0.3
10:34 am
BAN 73 74
10 Ov 44 44
0 0-0 0.2
10:33 am
BAN 73 74
10 Ov 44 45
0 0-0 0.1
10:32 am
BAN 73 74
10 Ov 45 45
Join the future with
AI-DRIVEN CRYPTO TOKENS ON BINANCE
DOWNLOAD APP
9:45
Live Scorecard Graphs Points Table
SA
428-5 (50.0)
SL
(44.5) 326-10
SA won by 102 runs
1 1-0 0.4
2:04 pm
SA 40 41
10 Ov 53 53
0 0-0 0.3
2:04 pm
SA 41 42
10 Ov 52 53
0 0-0 0.2
2:03 pm
SA 42 43
10 Ov 53 53
0 0-0 0.1
2:03 pm
SA 41 42
10 Ov 53 54

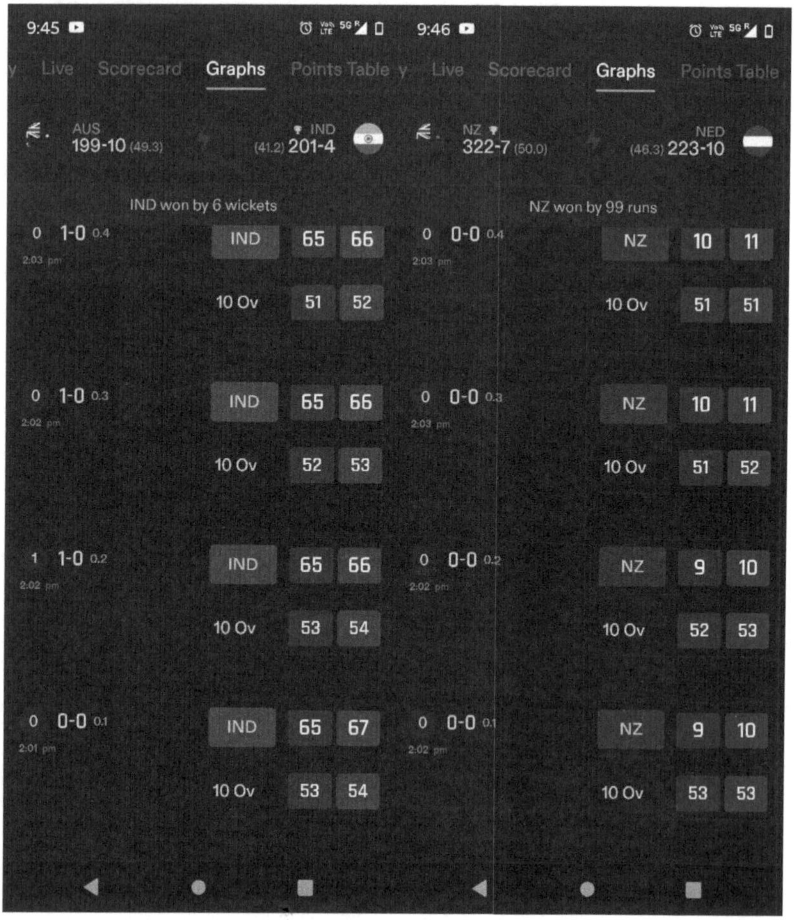
9:45
Live
Scorecard
Graphs
Points Table
AUS
199-10 (49.3)
IND
(41.2) 201-4
IND won by 6 wickets
0 1-0 0.4
2:03 pm
IND 65 66
10 Ov 51 52
0 1-0 0.3
2:02 pm
IND 65 66
10 Ov 52 53
1 1-0 0.2
2:02 pm
IND 65 66
10 Ov 53 54
0 0-0 0.1
2:01 pm
IND 65 67
10 Ov 53 54
9:46
Live
Scorecard
Graphs
Points Table
NZ
322-7 (50.0)
NED
(46.3) 223-10
NZ won by 99 runs
0 0-0 0.4
2:03 pm
NZ 10 11
10 Ov 51 51
0 0-0 0.3
2:03 pm
NZ 10 11
10 Ov 51 52
0 0-0 0.2
2:02 pm
NZ 9 10
10 Ov 52 53
0 0-0 0.1
2:02 pm
NZ 9 10
10 Ov 53 53

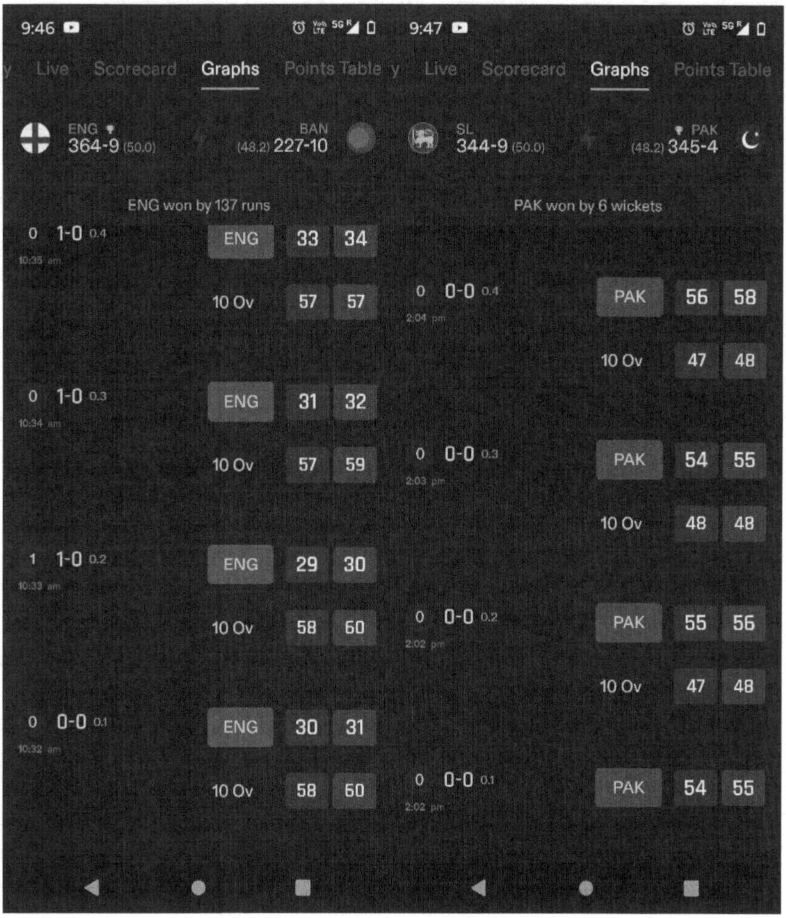

9:46
Live
Scorecard
Graphs
Points Table
ENG
364-9 (50.0)
BAN
(48.2) 227-10
ENG won by 137 runs
0 1-0 0.4
10:35 am
ENG 33 34
10 Ov 57 57
0 1-0 0.3
10:34 am
ENG 31 32
10 Ov 57 59
1 1-0 0.2
10:33 am
ENG 29 30
10 Ov 58 60
0 0-0 0.1
10:32 am
ENG 30 31
10 Ov 58 60
9:47
Live
Scorecard
Graphs
Points Table
SL
344-9 (50.0)
PAK
(48.2) 345-4
PAK won by 6 wickets
0 0-0 0.4
2:04 pm
PAK 56 58
10 Ov 47 48
0 0-0 0.3
2:03 pm
PAK 54 55
10 Ov 48 48
0 0-0 0.2
2:02 pm
PAK 55 56
10 Ov 47 48
0 0-0 0.1
2:02 pm
PAK 54 55

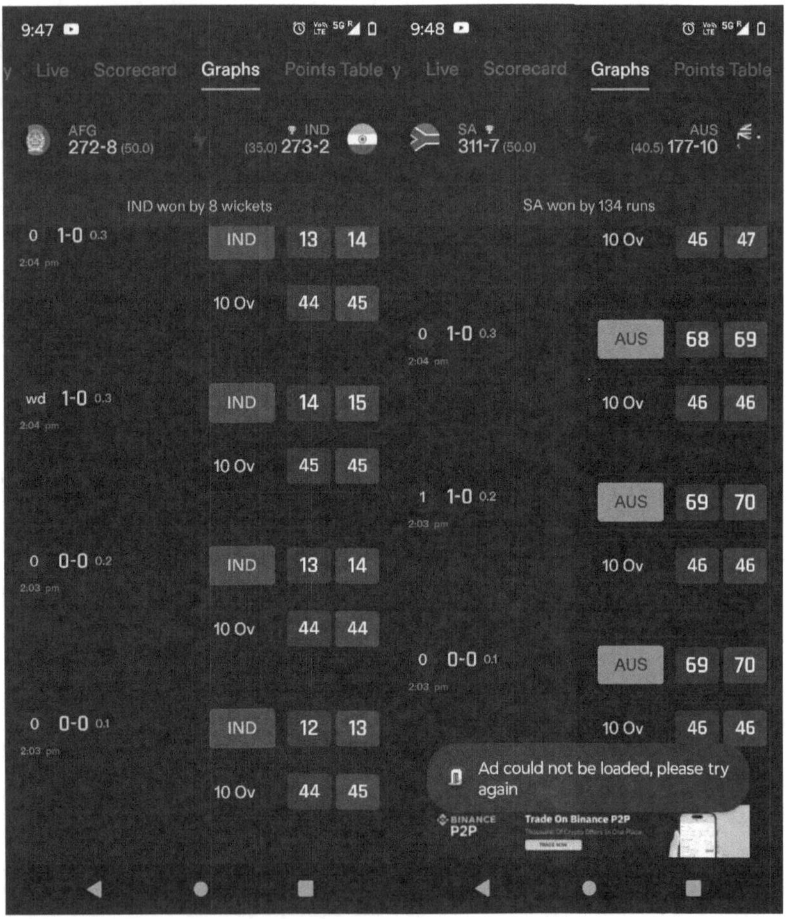
9:47
Live Scorecard Graphs Points Table
AFG 272-8 (50.0)
IND (35.0) 273-2
IND won by 8 wickets
0 1-0 0.3
2:04 pm
IND 13 14
10 Ov 44 45
wd 1-0 0.3
2:04 pm
IND 14 15
10 Ov 45 45
0 0-0 0.2
2:03 pm
IND 13 14
10 Ov 44 44
0 0-0 0.1
2:03 pm
IND 12 13
10 Ov 44 45
9:48
Live Scorecard Graphs Points Table
SA 311-7 (50.0)
AUS (40.5) 177-10
SA won by 134 runs
10 Ov 46 47
0 1-0 0.3
2:04 pm
AUS 68 69
10 Ov 46 46
1 1-0 0.2
2:03 pm
AUS 69 70
10 Ov 46 46
0 0-0 0.1
2:03 pm
AUS 69 70
10 Ov 46 46
Ad could not be loaded, please try again
BINANCE P2P
Trade On Binance P2P

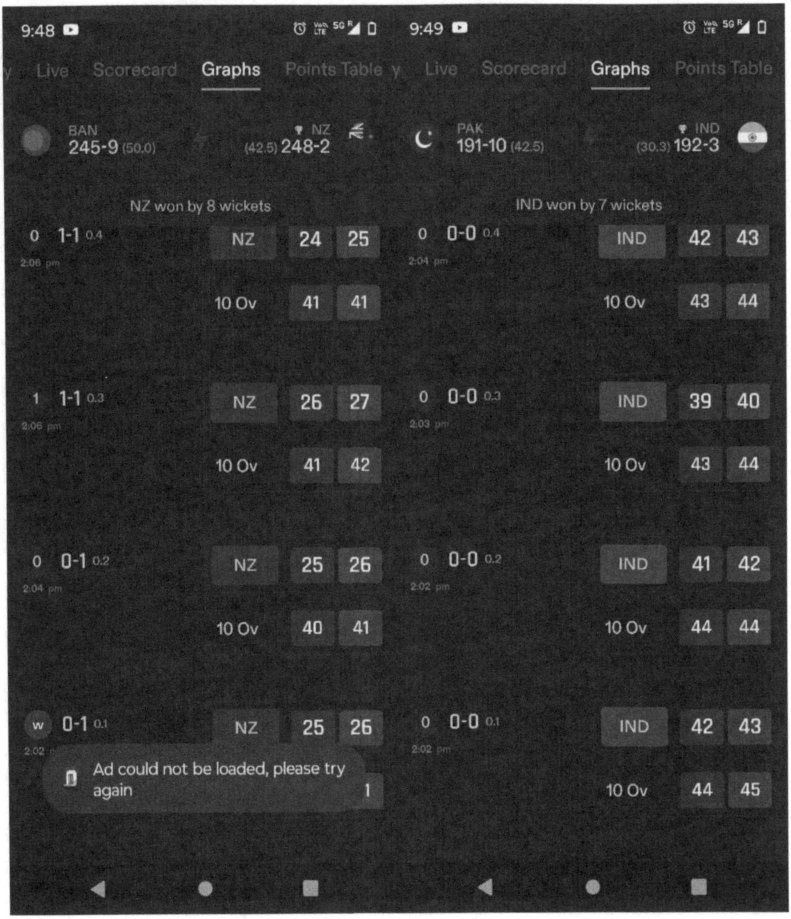
9:48
Live
Scorecard
Graphs
Points Table
BAN
245-9 (50.0)
NZ
(42.5) 248-2
NZ won by 8 wickets
0 1-1 0.4
2:06 pm
NZ 24 25
10 Ov 41 41
1 1-1 0.3
2:06 pm
NZ 26 27
10 Ov 41 42
0 0-1 0.2
2:04 pm
NZ 25 26
10 Ov 40 41
W 0-1 0.1
NZ 25 26
Ad could not be loaded, please try again
9:49
Live
Scorecard
Graphs
Points Table
PAK
191-10 (42.5)
IND
(30.3) 192-3
IND won by 7 wickets
0 0-0 0.4
2:04 pm
IND 42 43
10 Ov 43 44
0 0-0 0.3
2:03 pm
IND 39 40
10 Ov 43 44
0 0-0 0.2
2:02 pm
IND 41 42
10 Ov 44 44
0 0-0 0.1
2:02 pm
IND 42 43
10 Ov 44 45

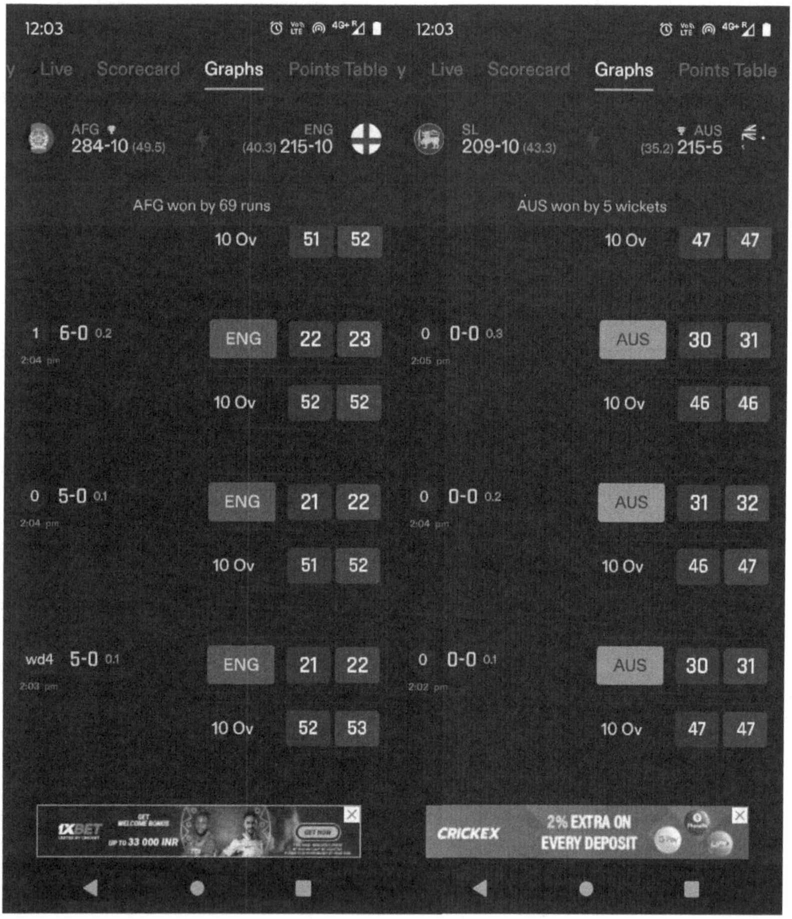
12:03
Live
Scorecard
Graphs
Points Table
AFG
284-10 (49.5)
ENG
(40.3) 215-10
AFG won by 69 runs
10 Ov 51 52
1 6-0 0.2
2:04 pm
ENG 22 23
10 Ov 52 52
0 5-0 0.1
2:04 pm
ENG 21 22
10 Ov 51 52
wd4 5-0 0.1
2:03 pm
ENG 21 22
10 Ov 52 53
1XBET
UP TO 33 000 INR
12:03
Live
Scorecard
Graphs
Points Table
SL
209-10 (43.3)
AUS
(35.2) 215-5
AUS won by 5 wickets
10 Ov 47 47
0 0-0 0.3
2:05 pm
AUS 30 31
10 Ov 46 46
0 0-0 0.2
2:04 pm
AUS 31 32
10 Ov 46 47
0 0-0 0.1
2:02 pm
AUS 30 31
10 Ov 47 47
CRICKEX
2% EXTRA ON
EVERY DEPOSIT

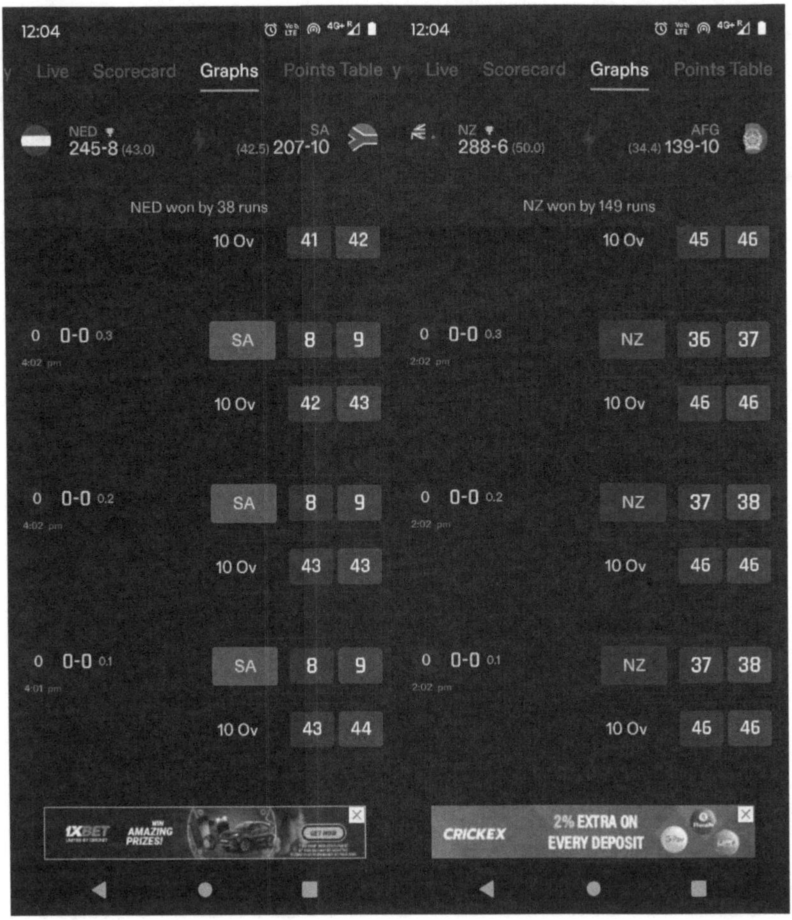
12:04
Live Scorecard Graphs Points Table
NED 245-8 (43.0)
SA (42.5) 207-10
NED won by 38 runs
10 Ov 41 42
0 0-0 0.3
4:02 pm
SA 8 9
10 Ov 42 43
0 0-0 0.2
4:02 pm
SA 8 9
10 Ov 43 43
0 0-0 0.1
4:01 pm
SA 8 9
10 Ov 43 44
1XBET
AMAZING PRIZES!
12:04
Live Scorecard Graphs Points Table
NZ 288-6 (50.0)
AFG (34.4) 139-10
NZ won by 149 runs
10 Ov 45 46
0 0-0 0.3
2:02 pm
NZ 36 37
10 Ov 46 46
0 0-0 0.2
2:02 pm
NZ 37 38
10 Ov 46 46
0 0-0 0.1
2:02 pm
NZ 37 38
10 Ov 46 46
CRICKEX
2% EXTRA ON EVERY DEPOSIT

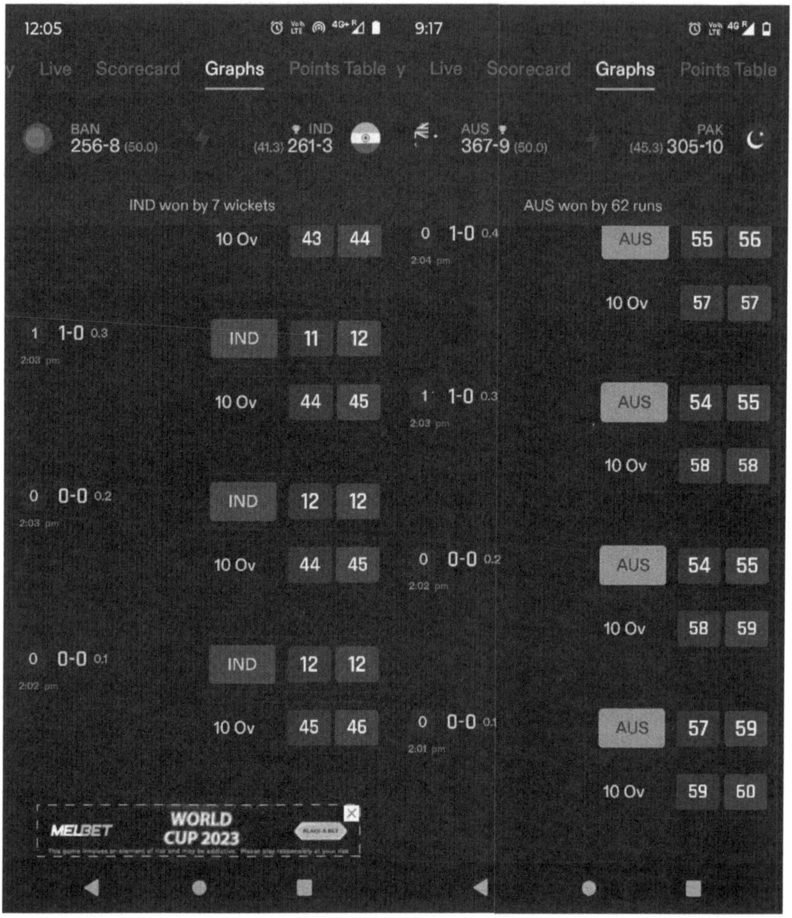
12:05
Live
Scorecard
Graphs
Points Table
BAN
256-8 (50.0)
IND
(41.3) 261-3
IND won by 7 wickets
10 Ov 43 44
1 1-0 0.3
2:03 pm
IND 11 12
10 Ov 44 45
0 0-0 0.2
2:03 pm
IND 12 12
10 Ov 44 45
0 0-0 0.1
2:02 pm
IND 12 12
10 Ov 45 46
MELBET
WORLD CUP 2023
9:17
Live
Scorecard
Graphs
Points Table
AUS
367-9 (50.0)
PAK
(45.3) 305-10
AUS won by 62 runs
0 1-0 0.4
2:04 pm
AUS 55 56
10 Ov 57 57
1 1-0 0.3
2:03 pm
AUS 54 55
10 Ov 58 58
0 0-0 0.2
2:02 pm
AUS 54 55
10 Ov 58 59
0 0-0 0.1
2:01 pm
AUS 57 59
10 Ov 59 60

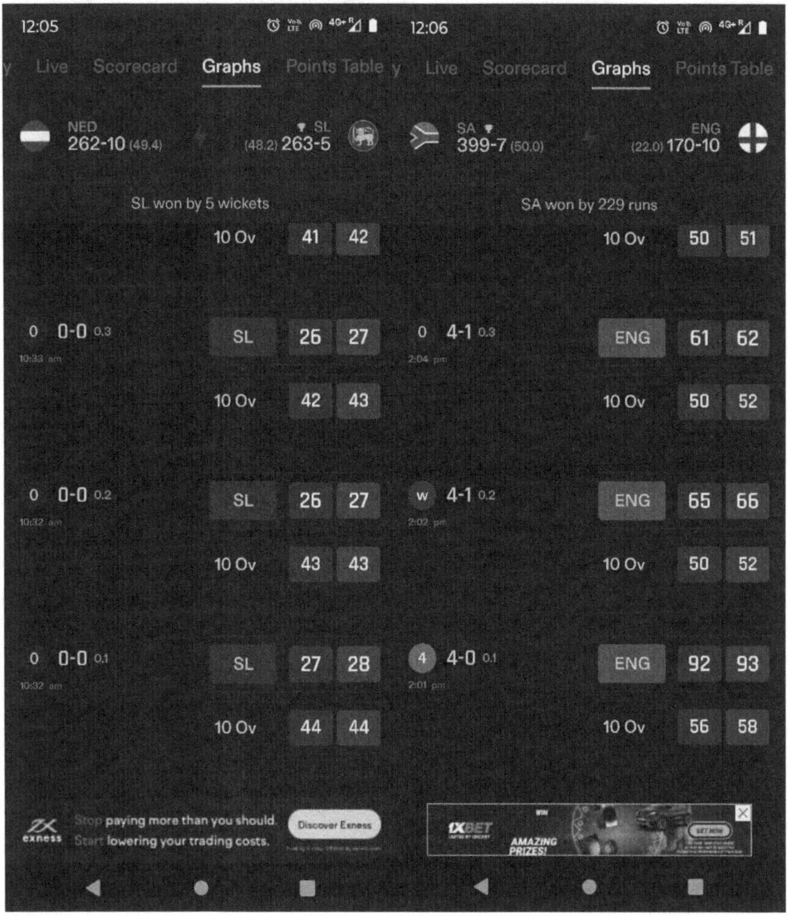
12:05
Live Scorecard Graphs Points Table
NED 262-10 (49.4)
SL (48.2) 263-5
SL won by 5 wickets
10 Ov 41 42
0 0-0 0.3
10:33 am
SL 26 27
10 Ov 42 43
0 0-0 0.2
10:32 am
SL 26 27
10 Ov 43 43
0 0-0 0.1
10:32 am
SL 27 28
10 Ov 44 44
exness
Stop paying more than you should.
Start lowering your trading costs.
Discover Exness
12:06
Live Scorecard Graphs Points Table
SA 399-7 (50.0)
ENG (22.0) 170-10
SA won by 229 runs
10 Ov 50 51
0 4-1 0.3
2:04 pm
ENG 61 62
10 Ov 50 52
W 4-1 0.2
2:02 pm
ENG 65 66
10 Ov 50 52
4 4-0 0.1
2:01 pm
ENG 92 93
10 Ov 56 58
1XBET
AMAZING PRIZES!

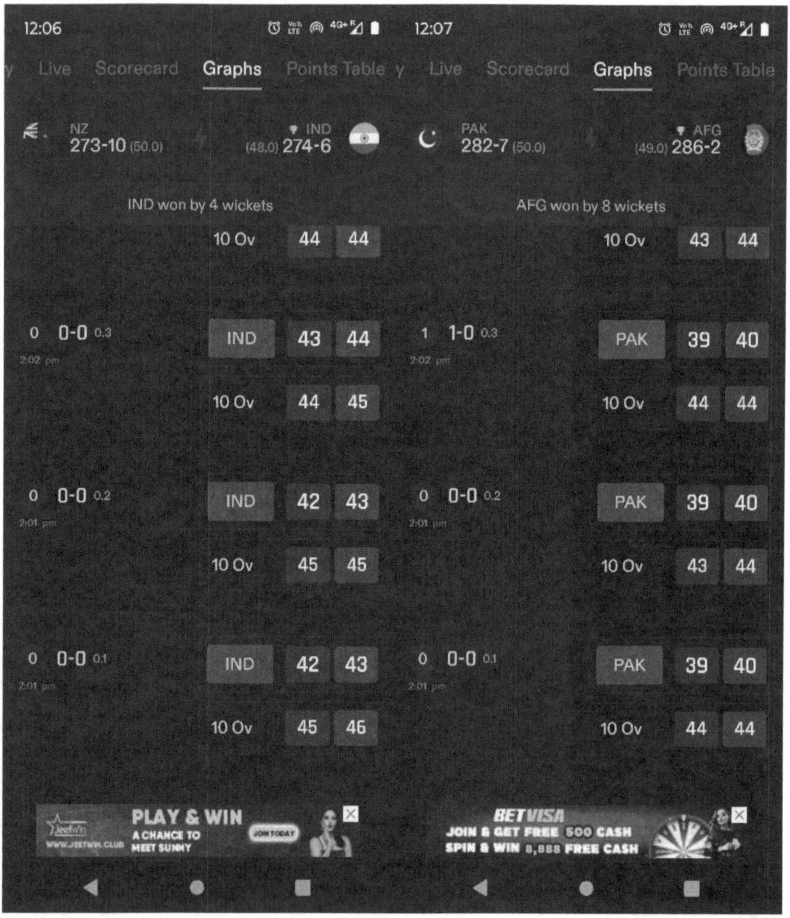
12:06
Live
Scorecard
Graphs
Points Table
NZ
273-10 (50.0)
IND
(48.0) 274-6
IND won by 4 wickets
10 Ov 44 44
0 0-0 0.3
2:02 pm
IND 43 44
10 Ov 44 45
0 0-0 0.2
2:01 pm
IND 42 43
10 Ov 45 45
0 0-0 0.1
2:01 pm
IND 42 43
10 Ov 45 46
PLAY & WIN
A CHANCE TO MEET SUNNY
12:07
Live
Scorecard
Graphs
Points Table
PAK
282-7 (50.0)
AFG
(49.0) 286-2
AFG won by 8 wickets
10 Ov 43 44
1 1-0 0.3
2:02 pm
PAK 39 40
10 Ov 44 44
0 0-0 0.2
2:01 pm
PAK 39 40
10 Ov 43 44
0 0-0 0.1
2:01 pm
PAK 39 40
10 Ov 44 44
BETVISA
JOIN & GET FREE 500 CASH
SPIN & WIN 8,888 FREE CASH

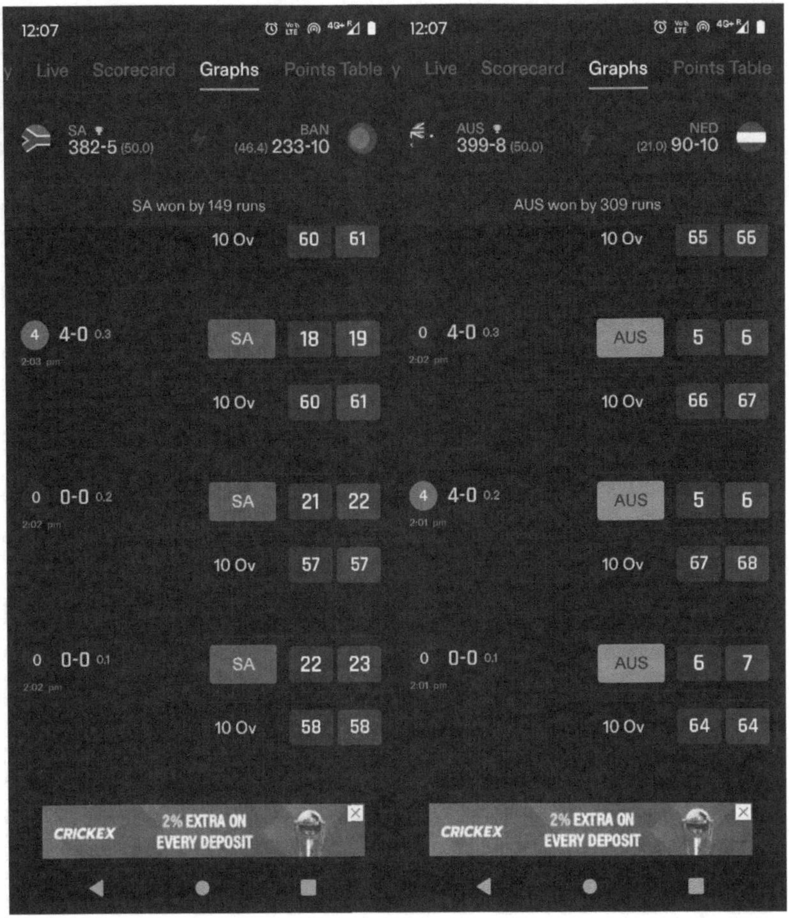
12:07
Live Scorecard Graphs Points Table
SA 382-5 (50.0)
BAN (46.4) 233-10
SA won by 149 runs
10 Ov 60 61
4 4-0 0.3
SA 18 19
10 Ov 60 61
0 0-0 0.2
SA 21 22
10 Ov 57 57
0 0-0 0.1
SA 22 23
10 Ov 58 58
CRICKEX 2% EXTRA ON EVERY DEPOSIT
12:07
Live Scorecard Graphs Points Table
AUS 399-8 (50.0)
NED (21.0) 90-10
AUS won by 309 runs
10 Ov 65 66
0 4-0 0.3
AUS 5 6
10 Ov 66 67
4 4-0 0.2
AUS 5 6
10 Ov 67 68
0 0-0 0.1
AUS 6 7
10 Ov 64 64
CRICKEX 2% EXTRA ON EVERY DEPOSIT

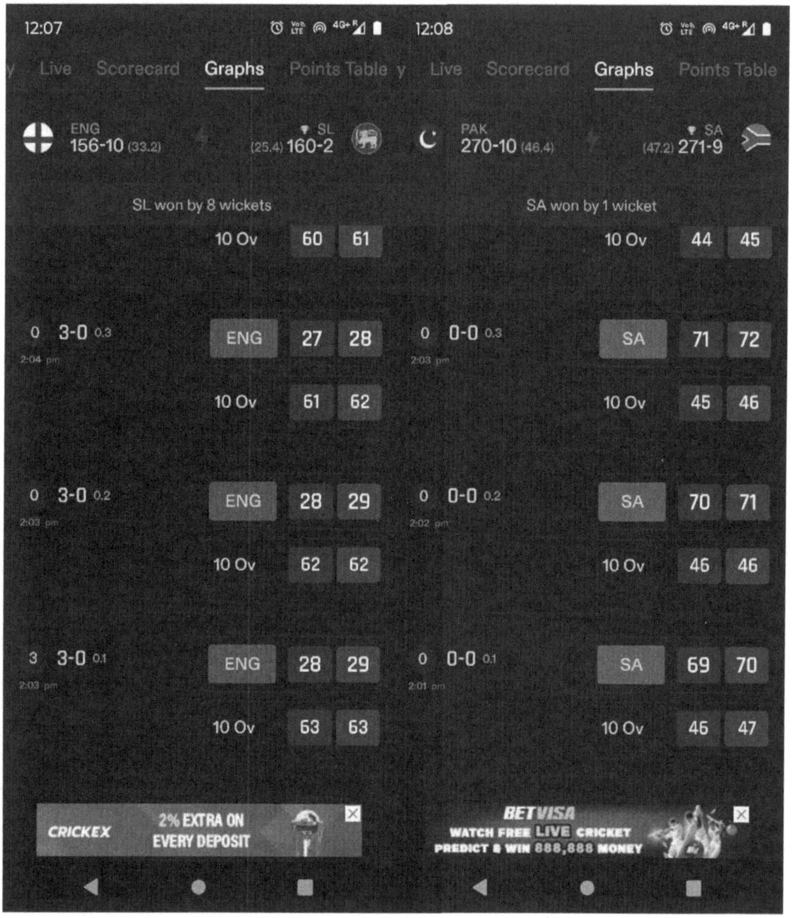
12:07
Live Scorecard Graphs Points Table
ENG
156-10 (33.2)
SL
(25.4) 160-2
SL won by 8 wickets
10 Ov 60 61
0 3-0 0.3
2:04 pm
ENG 27 28
10 Ov 61 62
0 3-0 0.2
2:03 pm
ENG 28 29
10 Ov 62 62
3 3-0 0.1
2:03 pm
ENG 28 29
10 Ov 63 63
CRICKEX
2% EXTRA ON EVERY DEPOSIT
12:08
Live Scorecard Graphs Points Table
PAK
270-10 (46.4)
SA
(47.2) 271-9
SA won by 1 wicket
10 Ov 44 45
0 0-0 0.3
2:03 pm
SA 71 72
10 Ov 45 46
0 0-0 0.2
2:02 pm
SA 70 71
10 Ov 46 46
0 0-0 0.1
2:01 pm
SA 69 70
10 Ov 46 47
BETVISA
WATCH FREE LIVE CRICKET
PREDICT & WIN 888,888 MONEY

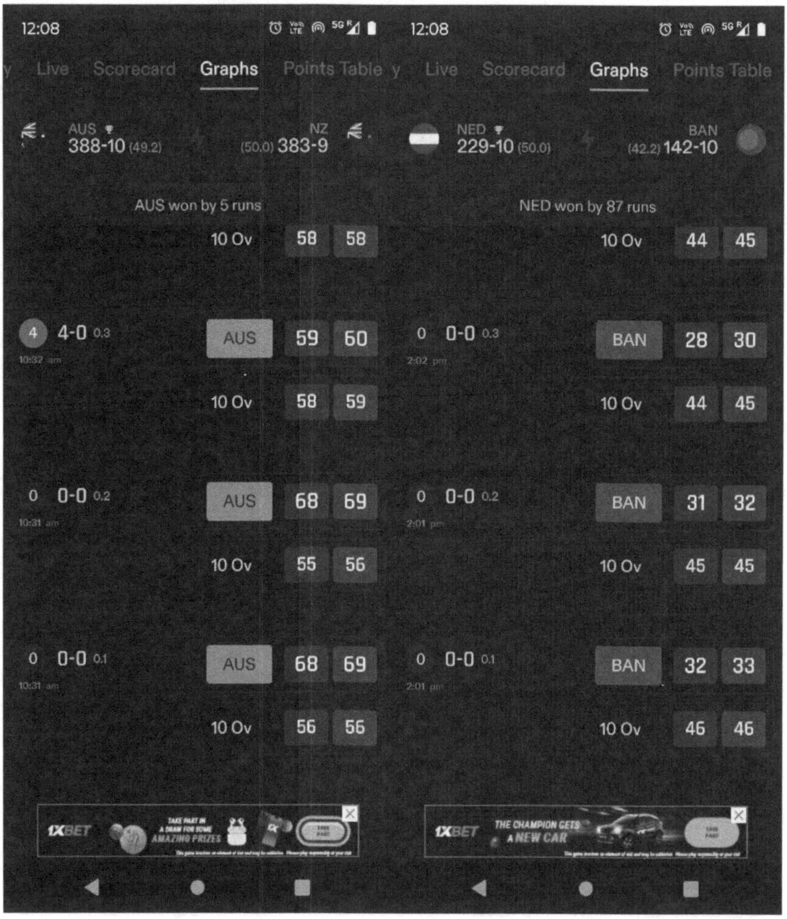
12:08
Live
Scorecard
Graphs
Points Table
AUS
388-10 (49.2)
NZ
(50.0) 383-9
AUS won by 5 runs
10 Ov 58 58
4 4-0 0.3
10:32 am
AUS 59 60
10 Ov 58 59
0 0-0 0.2
10:31 am
AUS 68 69
10 Ov 55 56
0 0-0 0.1
10:31 am
AUS 68 69
10 Ov 56 56
12:08
Live
Scorecard
Graphs
Points Table
NED
229-10 (50.0)
BAN
(42.2) 142-10
NED won by 87 runs
10 Ov 44 45
0 0-0 0.3
2:02 pm
BAN 28 30
10 Ov 44 45
0 0-0 0.2
2:01 pm
BAN 31 32
10 Ov 45 45
0 0-0 0.1
2:01 pm
BAN 32 33
10 Ov 46 46
1XBET
AMAZING PRIZES
1XBET
THE CHAMPION GETS A NEW CAR

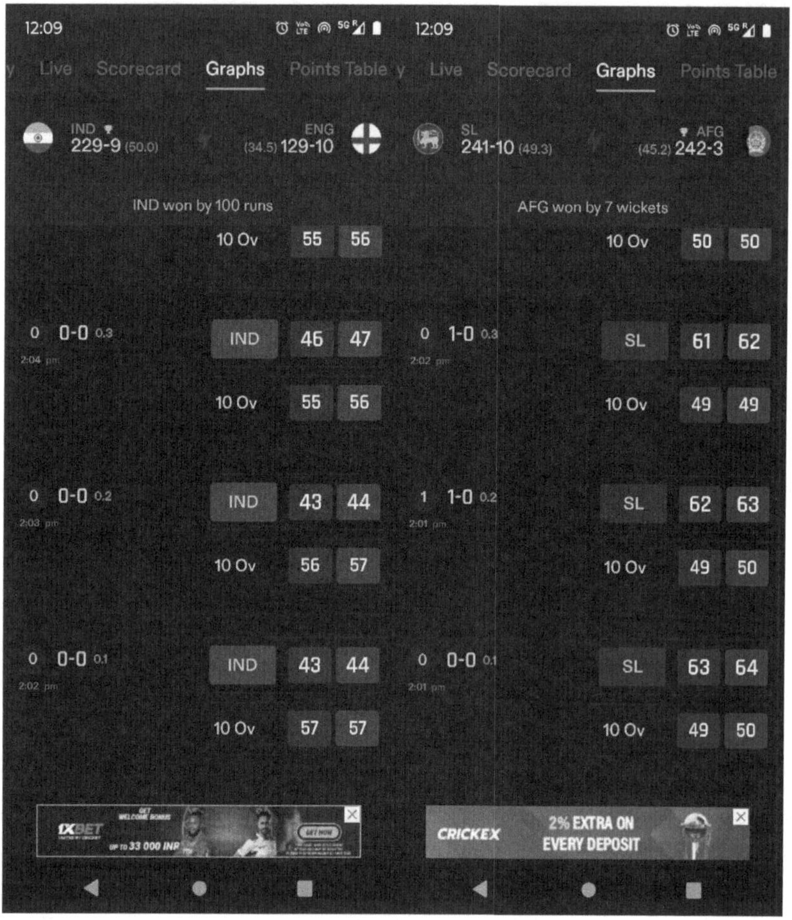
12:09
Live Scorecard Graphs Points Table
IND 229-9 (50.0)
ENG (34.5) 129-10
IND won by 100 runs
10 Ov 55 56
0 0-0 0.3
2:04 pm
IND 46 47
10 Ov 55 56
0 0-0 0.2
2:03 pm
IND 43 44
10 Ov 56 57
0 0-0 0.1
2:02 pm
IND 43 44
10 Ov 57 57
1XBET
UP TO 33 000 INR
12:09
Live Scorecard Graphs Points Table
SL 241-10 (49.3)
AFG (45.2) 242-3
AFG won by 7 wickets
10 Ov 50 50
0 1-0 0.3
2:02 pm
SL 61 62
10 Ov 49 49
1 1-0 0.2
2:01 pm
SL 62 63
10 Ov 49 50
0 0-0 0.1
2:01 pm
SL 63 64
10 Ov 49 50
CRICKEX
2% EXTRA ON EVERY DEPOSIT

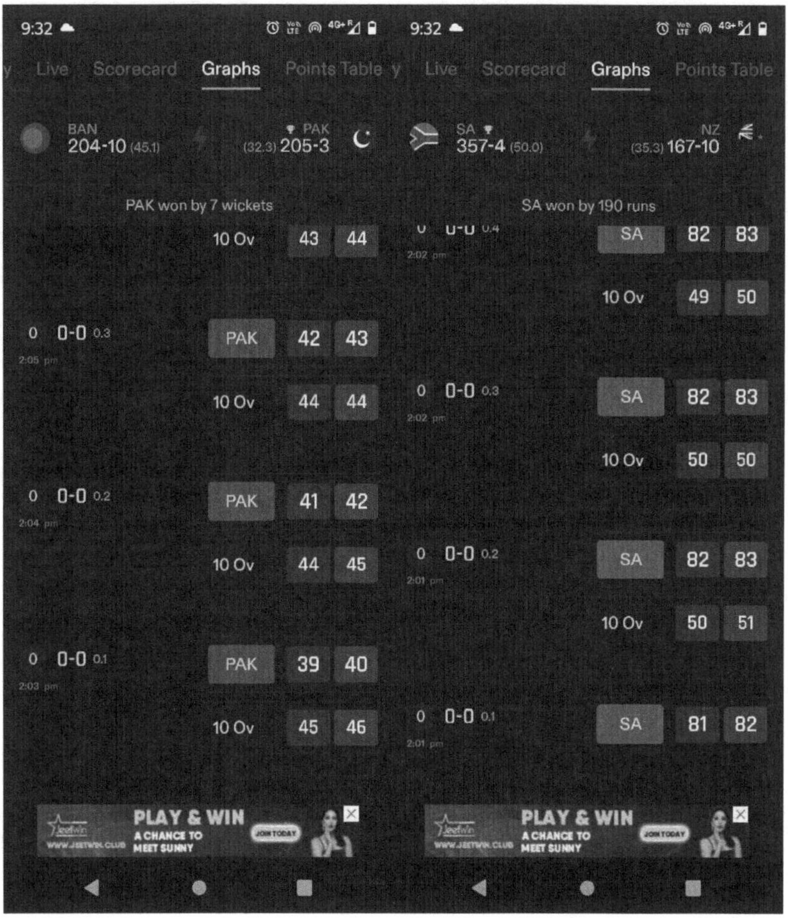
9:32
Live
Scorecard
Graphs
Points Table
BAN
204-10 (45.1)
PAK
(32.3) 205-3
PAK won by 7 wickets
10 Ov 43 44
0 0-0 0.3
2:05 pm
PAK 42 43
10 Ov 44 44
0 0-0 0.2
2:04 pm
PAK 41 42
10 Ov 44 45
0 0-0 0.1
2:03 pm
PAK 39 40
10 Ov 45 46
PLAY & WIN
A CHANCE TO MEET SUNNY
JOIN TODAY
9:32
Live
Scorecard
Graphs
Points Table
SA
357-4 (50.0)
NZ
(35.3) 167-10
SA won by 190 runs
2:02 pm
SA 82 83
10 Ov 49 50
0 0-0 0.3
2:02 pm
SA 82 83
10 Ov 50 50
0 0-0 0.2
2:01 pm
SA 82 83
10 Ov 50 51
0 0-0 0.1
2:01 pm
SA 81 82
PLAY & WIN
A CHANCE TO MEET SUNNY
JOIN TODAY

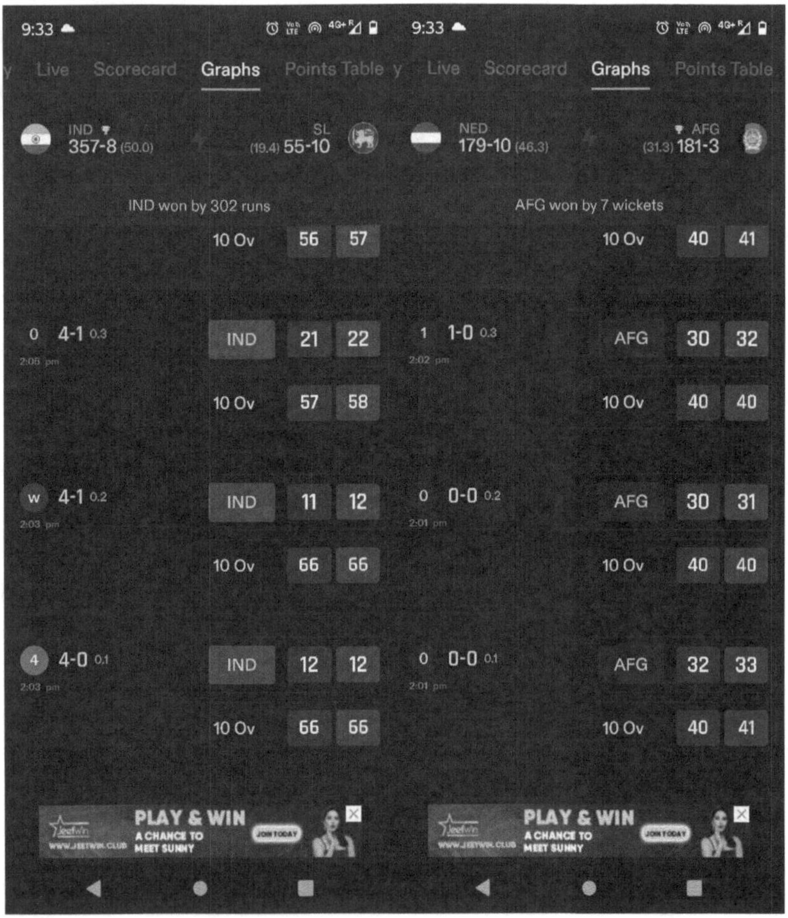
9:33
Live
Scorecard
Graphs
Points Table
IND
357-8 (50.0)
SL
(19.4) 55-10
IND won by 302 runs
10 Ov 56 57
0 4-1 0.3
IND 21 22
10 Ov 57 58
W 4-1 0.2
IND 11 12
10 Ov 66 66
4 4-0 0.1
IND 12 12
10 Ov 66 66
PLAY & WIN
A CHANCE TO MEET SUNNY
9:33
Live
Scorecard
Graphs
Points Table
NED
179-10 (46.3)
AFG
(31.3) 181-3
AFG won by 7 wickets
10 Ov 40 41
1 1-0 0.3
AFG 30 32
10 Ov 40 40
0 0-0 0.2
AFG 30 31
10 Ov 40 40
0 0-0 0.1
AFG 32 33
10 Ov 40 41
PLAY & WIN
A CHANCE TO MEET SUNNY

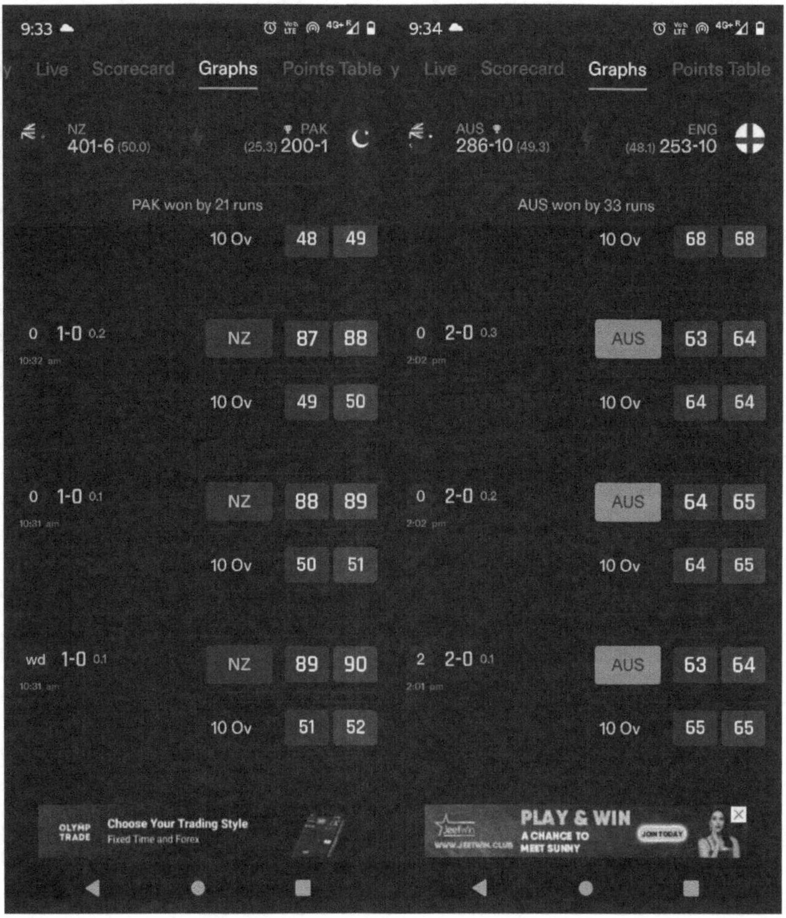
9:33
Live
Scorecard
Graphs
Points Table
NZ
401-6 (50.0)
PAK
(25.3) 200-1
PAK won by 21 runs
10 Ov 48 49
0 1-0 0.2
10:32 am
NZ 87 88
10 Ov 49 50
0 1-0 0.1
10:31 am
NZ 88 89
10 Ov 50 51
wd 1-0 0.1
10:31 am
NZ 89 90
10 Ov 51 52
OLYMP TRADE
Choose Your Trading Style
Fixed Time and Forex
9:34
Live
Scorecard
Graphs
Points Table
AUS
286-10 (49.3)
ENG
(48.1) 253-10
AUS won by 33 runs
10 Ov 68 68
0 2-0 0.3
2:02 pm
AUS 63 64
10 Ov 64 64
0 2-0 0.2
2:02 pm
AUS 64 65
10 Ov 64 65
2 2-0 0.1
2:01 pm
AUS 63 64
10 Ov 65 65
PLAY & WIN
A CHANCE TO
MEET SUNNY
JOIN TODAY

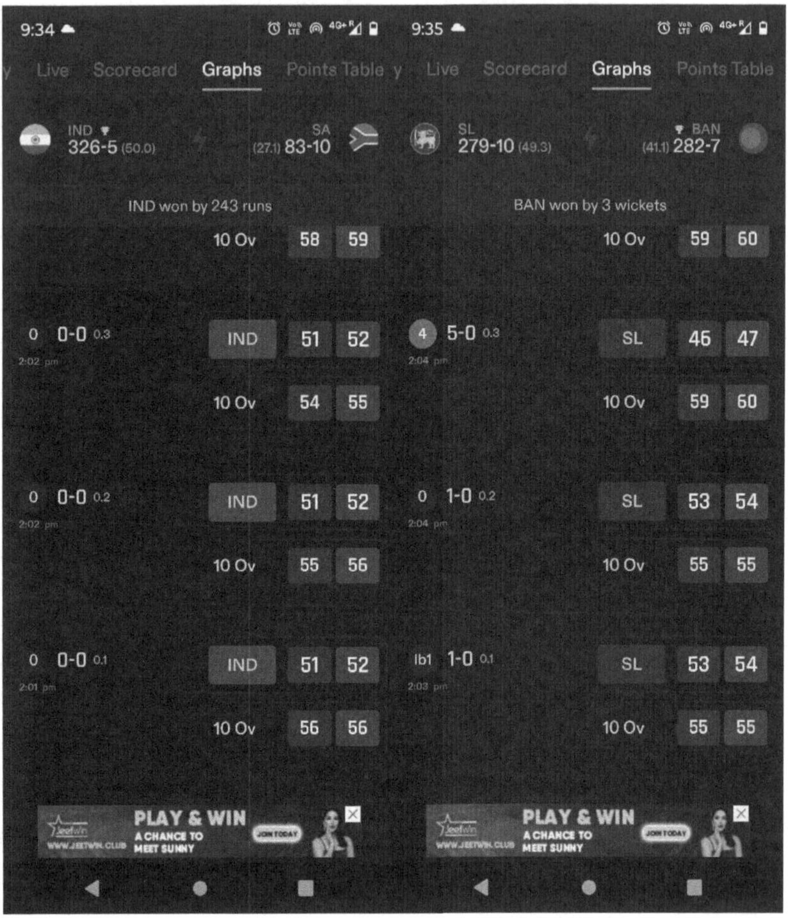
9:34
Live
Scorecard
Graphs
Points Table
IND
326-5 (50.0)
SA
(27.1) 83-10
IND won by 243 runs
10 Ov 58 59
0 0-0 0.3
2:02 pm
IND 51 52
10 Ov 54 55
0 0-0 0.2
2:02 pm
IND 51 52
10 Ov 55 56
0 0-0 0.1
2:01 pm
IND 51 52
10 Ov 56 56
PLAY & WIN
A CHANCE TO MEET SUNNY
9:35
Live
Scorecard
Graphs
Points Table
SL
279-10 (49.3)
BAN
(41.1) 282-7
BAN won by 3 wickets
10 Ov 59 60
4 5-0 0.3
2:04 pm
SL 46 47
10 Ov 59 60
0 1-0 0.2
2:04 pm
SL 53 54
10 Ov 55 55
lb1 1-0 0.1
2:03 pm
SL 53 54
10 Ov 55 55
PLAY & WIN
A CHANCE TO MEET SUNNY

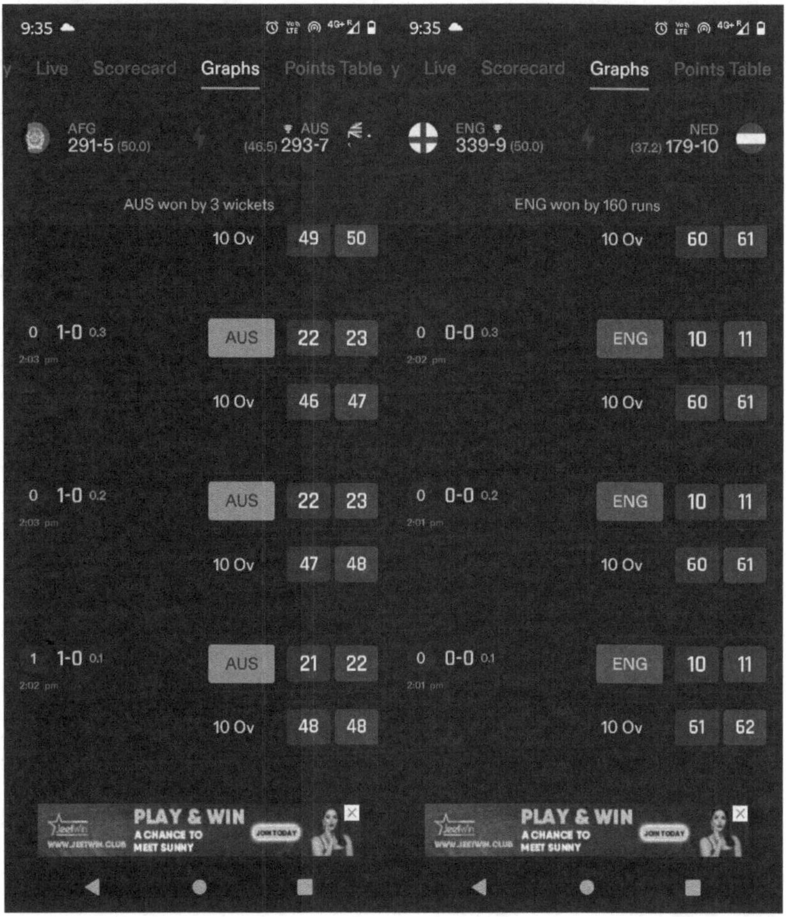
9:35
Live
Scorecard
Graphs
Points Table
AFG
291-5 (50.0)
AUS
(46.5) 293-7
AUS won by 3 wickets
10 Ov 49 50
0 1-0 0.3
2:03 pm
AUS 22 23
10 Ov 46 47
0 1-0 0.2
2:03 pm
AUS 22 23
10 Ov 47 48
1 1-0 0.1
2:02 pm
AUS 21 22
10 Ov 48 48
PLAY & WIN
A CHANCE TO MEET SUNNY
JOIN TODAY
9:35
Live
Scorecard
Graphs
Points Table
ENG
339-9 (50.0)
NED
(37.2) 179-10
ENG won by 160 runs
10 Ov 60 61
0 0-0 0.3
2:02 pm
ENG 10 11
10 Ov 60 61
0 0-0 0.2
2:01 pm
ENG 10 11
10 Ov 60 61
0 0-0 0.1
2:01 pm
ENG 10 11
10 Ov 61 62
PLAY & WIN
A CHANCE TO MEET SUNNY
JOIN TODAY

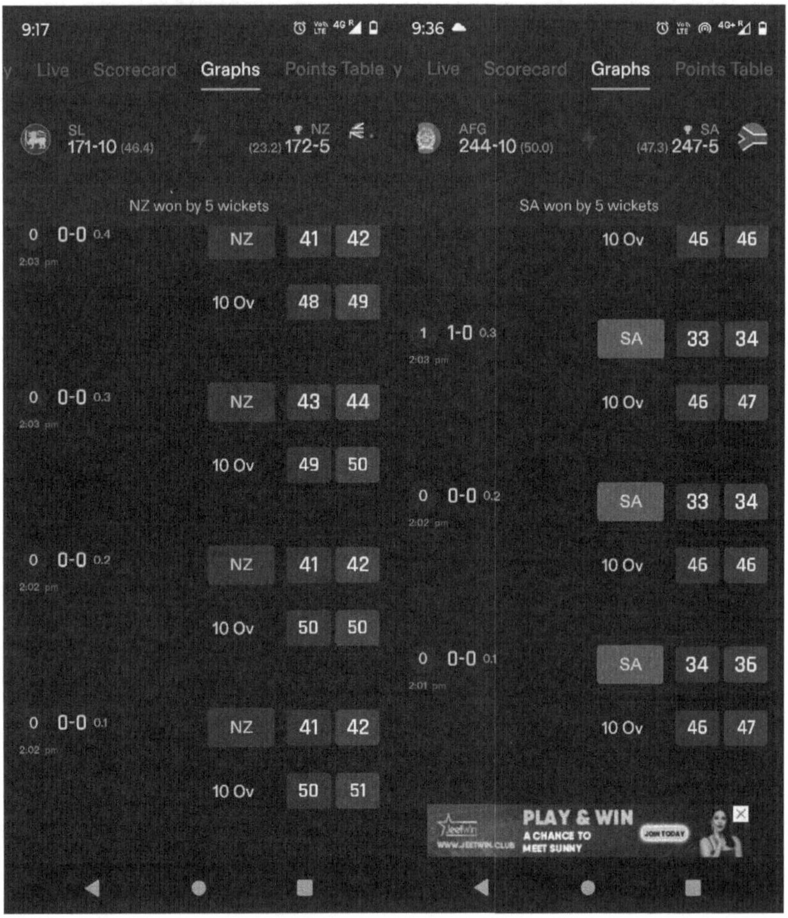
9:17
Live
Scorecard
Graphs
Points Table
SL
171-10 (46.4)
NZ
(23.2) 172-5
NZ won by 5 wickets
0 0-0 0.4
2:03 pm
NZ 41 42
10 Ov 48 49
0 0-0 0.3
2:03 pm
NZ 43 44
10 Ov 49 50
0 0-0 0.2
2:02 pm
NZ 41 42
10 Ov 50 50
0 0-0 0.1
2:02 pm
NZ 41 42
10 Ov 50 51
9:36
Live
Scorecard
Graphs
Points Table
AFG
244-10 (50.0)
SA
(47.3) 247-5
SA won by 5 wickets
10 Ov 46 46
1 1-0 0.3
2:03 pm
SA 33 34
10 Ov 46 47
0 0-0 0.2
2:02 pm
SA 33 34
10 Ov 46 46
0 0-0 0.1
2:01 pm
SA 34 36
10 Ov 46 47
PLAY & WIN
A CHANCE TO MEET SUNNY
JOIN TODAY

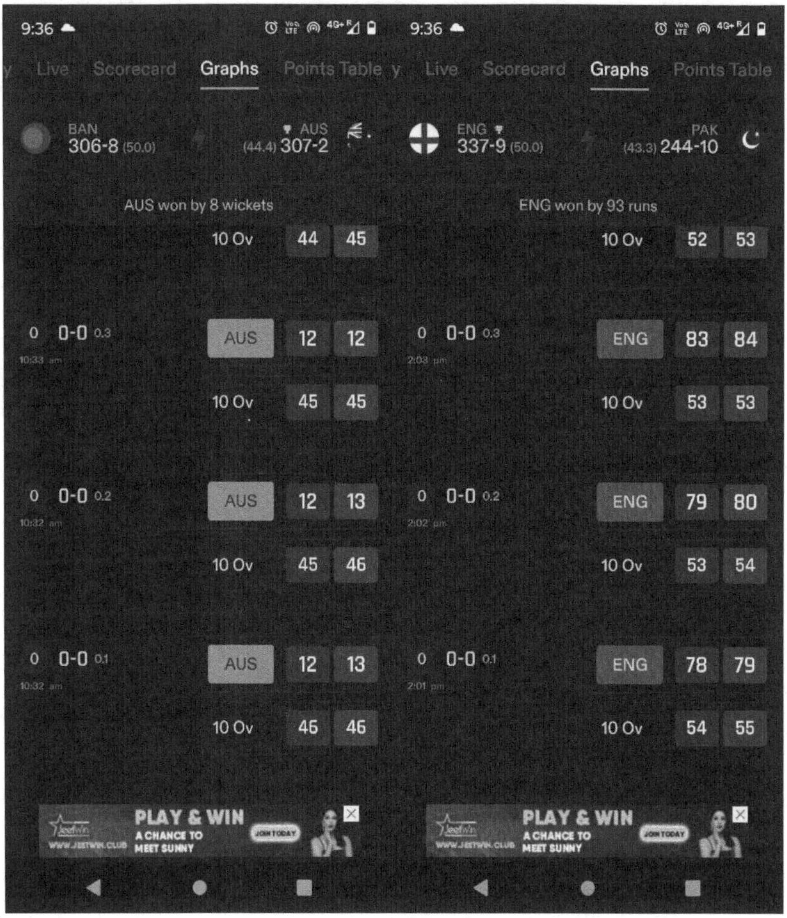
9:36
Live
Scorecard
Graphs
Points Table
BAN
306-8 (50.0)
AUS
(44.4) 307-2
AUS won by 8 wickets
10 Ov 44 45
0 0-0 0.3
10:33 am
AUS 12 12
10 Ov 45 45
0 0-0 0.2
10:32 am
AUS 12 13
10 Ov 45 46
0 0-0 0.1
10:32 am
AUS 12 13
10 Ov 46 46
PLAY & WIN
A CHANCE TO MEET SUNNY
9:36
Live
Scorecard
Graphs
Points Table
ENG
337-9 (50.0)
PAK
(43.3) 244-10
ENG won by 93 runs
10 Ov 52 53
0 0-0 0.3
2:03 pm
ENG 83 84
10 Ov 53 53
0 0-0 0.2
2:02 pm
ENG 79 80
10 Ov 53 54
0 0-0 0.1
2:01 pm
ENG 78 79
10 Ov 54 55
PLAY & WIN
A CHANCE TO MEET SUNNY

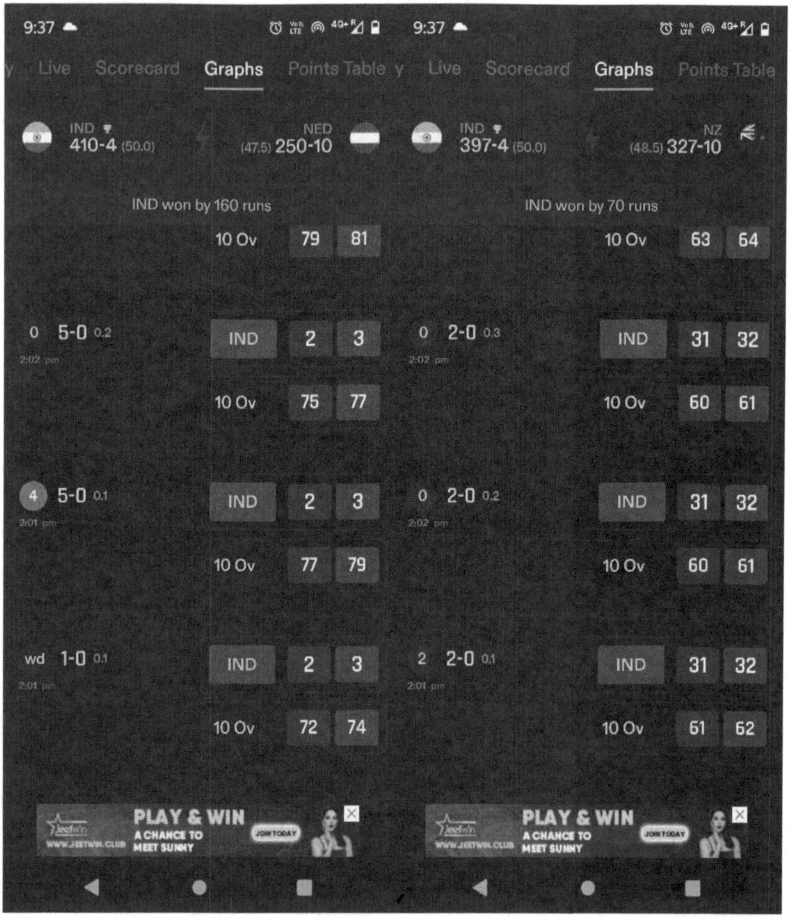
9:37
Live
Scorecard
Graphs
Points Table
IND
410-4 (50.0)
NED
(47.5) 250-10
IND won by 160 runs
10 Ov 79 81
0 5-0 0.2
2:02 pm
IND 2 3
10 Ov 75 77
4 5-0 0.1
2:01 pm
IND 2 3
10 Ov 77 79
wd 1-0 0.1
2:01 pm
IND 2 3
10 Ov 72 74
PLAY & WIN
A CHANCE TO MEET SUNNY
JOIN TODAY
9:37
Live
Scorecard
Graphs
Points Table
IND
397-4 (50.0)
NZ
(48.5) 327-10
IND won by 70 runs
10 Ov 63 64
0 2-0 0.3
2:02 pm
IND 31 32
10 Ov 60 61
0 2-0 0.2
2:02 pm
IND 31 32
10 Ov 60 61
2 2-0 0.1
2:01 pm
IND 31 32
10 Ov 61 62
PLAY & WIN
A CHANCE TO MEET SUNNY
JOIN TODAY

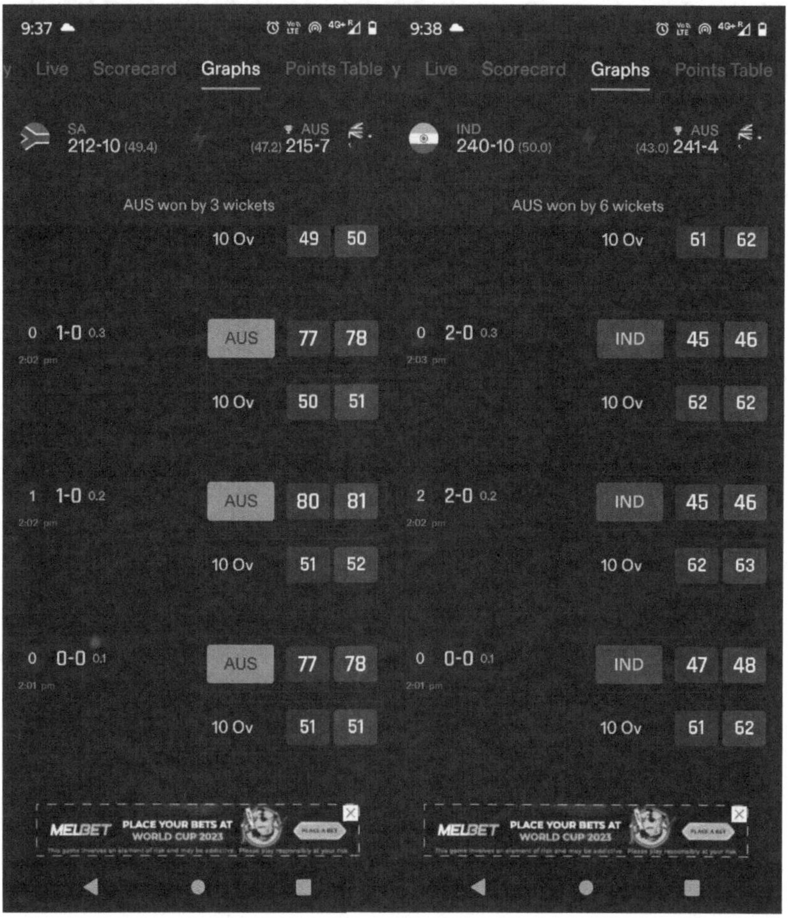
9:37
Live
Scorecard
Graphs
Points Table
SA
212-10 (49.4)
AUS
(47.2) 215-7
AUS won by 3 wickets
10 Ov 49 50
0 1-0 0.3
2:02 pm
AUS 77 78
10 Ov 50 51
1 1-0 0.2
2:02 pm
AUS 80 81
10 Ov 51 52
0 0-0 0.1
2:01 pm
AUS 77 78
10 Ov 51 51
MELBET PLACE YOUR BETS AT WORLD CUP 2023
9:38
Live
Scorecard
Graphs
Points Table
IND
240-10 (50.0)
AUS
(43.0) 241-4
AUS won by 6 wickets
10 Ov 61 62
0 2-0 0.3
2:03 pm
IND 45 46
10 Ov 62 62
2 2-0 0.2
2:02 pm
IND 45 46
10 Ov 62 63
0 0-0 0.1
2:01 pm
IND 47 48
10 Ov 61 62
MELBET PLACE YOUR BETS AT WORLD CUP 2023

The following screenshots from another app give a record of the starting sessions for all the matches in the CWC 2023. Under the column 'Open' the session scores are given; these are the scores for backing at the start of the given session (number of overs for a session are indicated in the extreme left column). Under the column 'Pass' on the right are the scores achieved at the end of that session. The opening session score given for a session generally should be/is after the previous session ended.

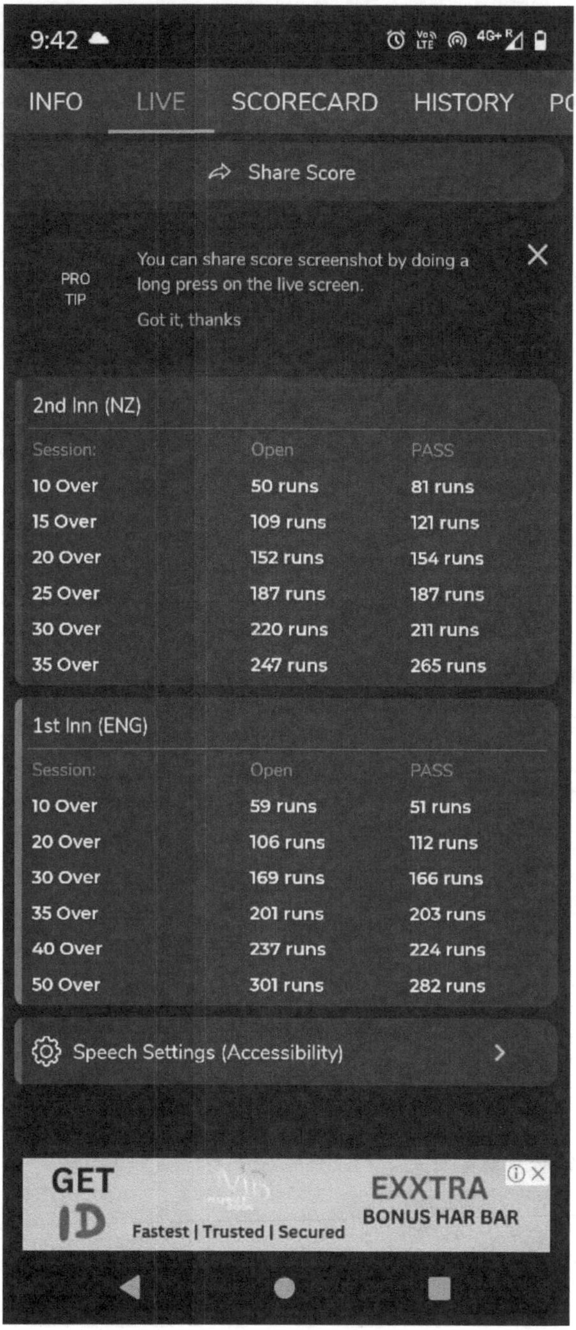
9:42
INFO
LIVE
SCORECARD
HISTORY
Share Score
PRO TIP
You can share score screenshot by doing a long press on the live screen.
Got it, thanks
2nd Inn (NZ)
Session: Open PASS
10 Over 50 runs 81 runs
15 Over 109 runs 121 runs
20 Over 152 runs 154 runs
25 Over 187 runs 187 runs
30 Over 220 runs 211 runs
35 Over 247 runs 265 runs
1st Inn (ENG)
Session: Open PASS
10 Over 59 runs 51 runs
20 Over 106 runs 112 runs
30 Over 169 runs 166 runs
35 Over 201 runs 203 runs
40 Over 237 runs 224 runs
50 Over 301 runs 282 runs
Speech Settings (Accessibility)
GET ID
Fastest | Trusted | Secured
EXXTRA
BONUS HAR BAR

9:46
INFO
LIVE
SCORECARD
HISTORY
Econ: 4.78
Rauf's last over: 0.1.0.0.4.1|1.1.0.1.0.0
Share Score
PRO TIP
You can share score screenshot by doing a long press on the live screen.
Got it, thanks
2nd Inn (NED)
Session: Open PASS
10 Over 45 runs 47 runs
15 Over 72 runs 60 runs
20 Over 84 runs 98 runs
25 Over 129 runs 125 runs
30 Over 151 runs 150 runs
35 Over 176 runs 174 runs
1st Inn (PAK)
Session: Open PASS
10 Over 55 runs 43 runs
20 Over 90 runs 101 runs
30 Over 154 runs 170 runs
35 Over 200 runs 196 runs
40 Over 224 runs 227 runs
50 Over 302 runs 286 runs
Speech Settings (Accessibility)

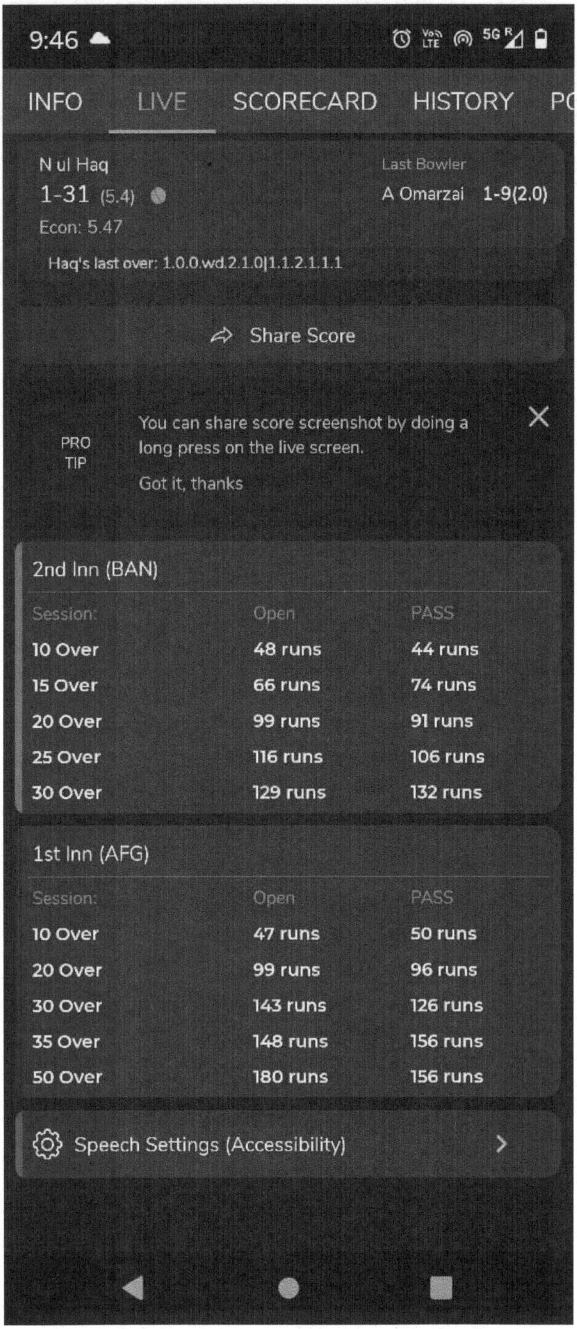
9:46
INFO
LIVE
SCORECARD
HISTORY
N ul Haq
1-31 (5.4)
Econ: 5.47
Last Bowler
A Omarzai 1-9(2.0)
Haq's last over: 1.0.0.wd.2.1.0|1.1.2.1.1.1
Share Score
PRO TIP
You can share score screenshot by doing a long press on the live screen.
Got it, thanks
2nd Inn (BAN)
Session: Open PASS
10 Over 48 runs 44 runs
15 Over 66 runs 74 runs
20 Over 99 runs 91 runs
25 Over 116 runs 106 runs
30 Over 129 runs 132 runs
1st Inn (AFG)
Session: Open PASS
10 Over 47 runs 50 runs
20 Over 99 runs 96 runs
30 Over 143 runs 126 runs
35 Over 148 runs 156 runs
50 Over 180 runs 156 runs
Speech Settings (Accessibility)

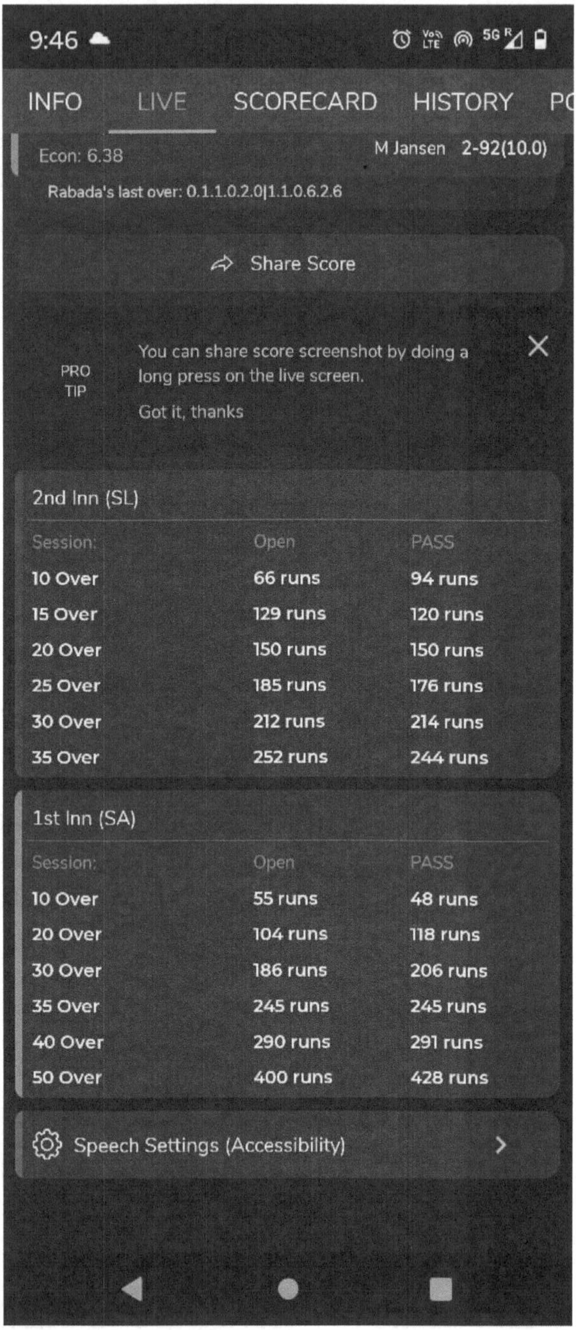
9:46
INFO
LIVE
SCORECARD
HISTORY
Econ: 6.38
M Jansen 2-92(10.0)
Rabada's last over: 0.1.1.0.2.0|1.1.0.6.2.6
Share Score
PRO TIP
You can share score screenshot by doing a long press on the live screen.
Got it, thanks
2nd Inn (SL)
Session: Open PASS
10 Over 66 runs 94 runs
15 Over 129 runs 120 runs
20 Over 150 runs 150 runs
25 Over 185 runs 176 runs
30 Over 212 runs 214 runs
35 Over 252 runs 244 runs
1st Inn (SA)
Session: Open PASS
10 Over 55 runs 48 runs
20 Over 104 runs 118 runs
30 Over 186 runs 206 runs
35 Over 245 runs 245 runs
40 Over 290 runs 291 runs
50 Over 400 runs 428 runs
Speech Settings (Accessibility)

9:47
INFO
LIVE
SCORECARD
HISTORY
Share Score
PRO TIP
You can share score screenshot by doing a long press on the live screen.
Got it, thanks
2nd Inn (IND)
Session: Open PASS
10 Over 49 runs 27 runs
15 Over 50 runs 49 runs
20 Over 73 runs 80 runs
25 Over 106 runs 97 runs
30 Over 124 runs 120 runs
35 Over 148 runs 151 runs
40 Over 184 runs 182 runs
1st Inn (AUS)
Session: Open PASS
10 Over 57 runs 43 runs
20 Over 94 runs 85 runs
30 Over 138 runs 119 runs
35 Over 142 runs 138 runs
40 Over 166 runs 156 runs
50 Over 198 runs 199 runs
Speech Settings (Accessibility)
NoBroker Rent Pay
Fast and Secure Rent Payments
VISIT SITE

9:47
INFO
LIVE
SCORECARD
HISTORY
Share Score
PRO TIP
You can share score screenshot by doing a long press on the live screen.
Got it, thanks
2nd Inn (NED)
Session: Open PASS
10 Over 47 runs 35 runs
15 Over 59 runs 62 runs
20 Over 86 runs 80 runs
25 Over 106 runs 114 runs
30 Over 142 runs 145 runs
35 Over 178 runs 174 runs
40 Over 199 runs 196 runs
1st Inn (NZ)
Session: Open PASS
10 Over 57 runs 63 runs
20 Over 129 runs 102 runs
30 Over 165 runs 171 runs
35 Over 208 runs 198 runs
40 Over 233 runs 238 runs
50 Over 336 runs 322 runs
Speech Settings (Accessibility)
NoBroker Rent Pay
Fast and Secure Rent Payments
VISIT SITE

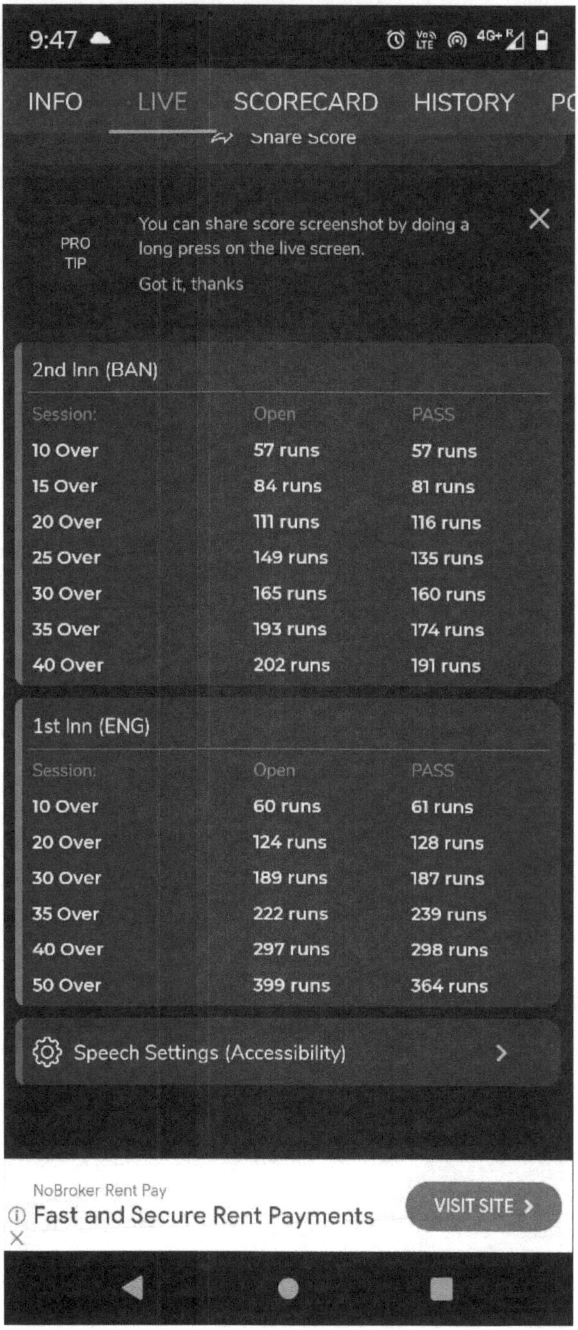
9:47
INFO
LIVE
SCORECARD
HISTORY
Share Score
PRO TIP
You can share score screenshot by doing a long press on the live screen.
Got it, thanks
2nd Inn (BAN)
Session: Open PASS
10 Over 57 runs 57 runs
15 Over 84 runs 81 runs
20 Over 111 runs 116 runs
25 Over 149 runs 135 runs
30 Over 165 runs 160 runs
35 Over 193 runs 174 runs
40 Over 202 runs 191 runs
1st Inn (ENG)
Session: Open PASS
10 Over 60 runs 61 runs
20 Over 124 runs 128 runs
30 Over 189 runs 187 runs
35 Over 222 runs 239 runs
40 Over 297 runs 298 runs
50 Over 399 runs 364 runs
Speech Settings (Accessibility)
NoBroker Rent Pay
Fast and Secure Rent Payments
VISIT SITE

9:47
INFO
LIVE
SCORECARD
HISTORY
Share Score
PRO TIP
You can share score screenshot by doing a long press on the live screen.
Got it, thanks
2nd Inn (PAK)
Session: Open PASS
10 Over 58 runs 48 runs
15 Over 76 runs 71 runs
20 Over 105 runs 110 runs
25 Over 148 runs 138 runs
30 Over 176 runs 182 runs
35 Over 222 runs 228 runs
40 Over 262 runs 271 runs
1st Inn (SL)
Session: Open PASS
10 Over 48 runs 58 runs
20 Over 110 runs 127 runs
30 Over 182 runs 229 runs
35 Over 259 runs 247 runs
40 Over 280 runs 283 runs
50 Over 370 runs 344 runs
Speech Settings (Accessibility)
NoBroker Rent Pay
Fast and Secure Rent Payments
VISIT SITE

9:47
INFO
LIVE
SCORECARD
HISTORY
Share Score
PRO TIP
You can share score screenshot by doing a long press on the live screen.
Got it, thanks
2nd Inn (IND)
Session: Open PASS
10 Over 95 runs 94 runs
15 Over 130 runs 130 runs
20 Over 163 runs 164 runs
25 Over 202 runs 202 runs
30 Over 245 runs 237 runs
1st Inn (AFG)
Session: Open PASS
10 Over 47 runs 48 runs
20 Over 98 runs 83 runs
30 Over 129 runs 147 runs
35 Over 177 runs 189 runs
40 Over 219 runs 211 runs
50 Over 292 runs 272 runs
Speech Settings (Accessibility)
50% · 5%
MEGA XTRAA EVERYTIME
NO ROLLINGG
GET ID
FINAL
(TRUSTED | SECURE | SAFE)

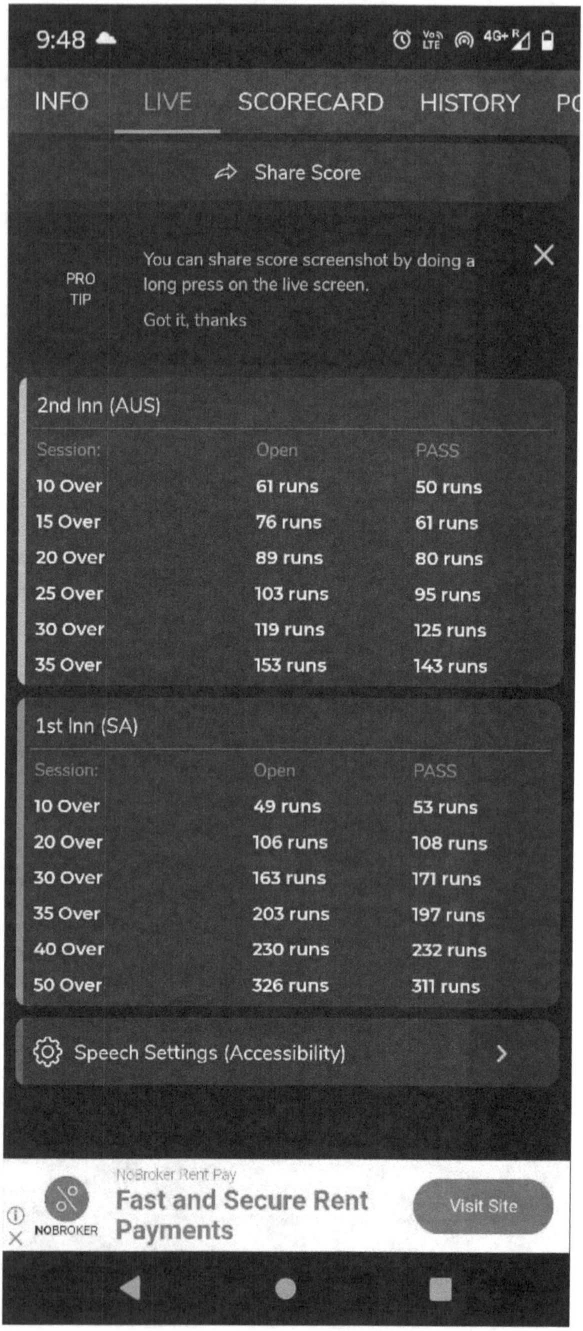
9:48
INFO
LIVE
SCORECARD
HISTORY
Share Score
PRO TIP
You can share score screenshot by doing a long press on the live screen.
Got it, thanks
2nd Inn (AUS)
Session: Open PASS
10 Over 61 runs 50 runs
15 Over 76 runs 61 runs
20 Over 89 runs 80 runs
25 Over 103 runs 95 runs
30 Over 119 runs 125 runs
35 Over 153 runs 143 runs
1st Inn (SA)
Session: Open PASS
10 Over 49 runs 53 runs
20 Over 106 runs 108 runs
30 Over 163 runs 171 runs
35 Over 203 runs 197 runs
40 Over 230 runs 232 runs
50 Over 326 runs 311 runs
Speech Settings (Accessibility)
NoBroker Rent Pay
Fast and Secure Rent Payments
NOBROKER
Visit Site

9:48
INFO
LIVE
SCORECARD
HISTORY
Share Score
PRO TIP
You can share score screenshot by doing a long press on the live screen.
Got it, thanks
2nd Inn (NZ)
Session: Open PASS
10 Over 53 runs 37 runs
15 Over 63 runs 68 runs
20 Over 95 runs 92 runs
25 Over 120 runs 123 runs
30 Over 152 runs 146 runs
35 Over 178 runs 174 runs
40 Over 209 runs 221 runs
1st Inn (BAN)
Session: Open PASS
10 Over 45 runs 46 runs
20 Over 91 runs 93 runs
30 Over 143 runs 152 runs
35 Over 177 runs 168 runs
40 Over 197 runs 189 runs
50 Over 231 runs 245 runs
Speech Settings (Accessibility)
NoBroker Rent Pay
Fast and Secure Rent Payments
NOBROKER
Visit Site

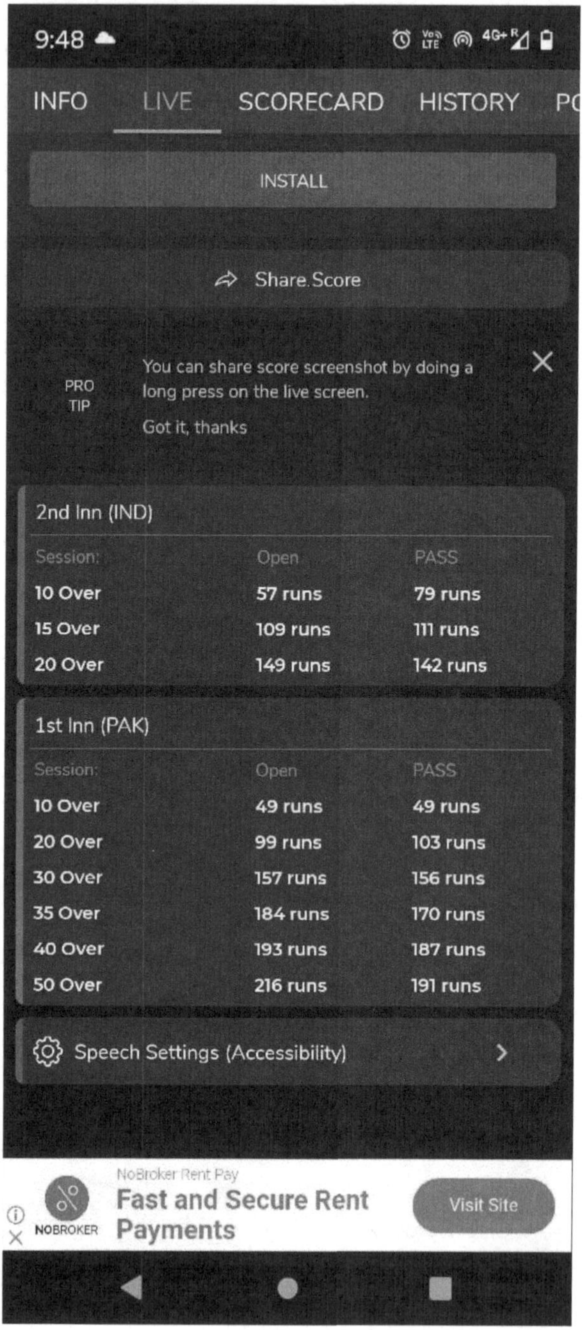
9:48
INFO
LIVE
SCORECARD
HISTORY
INSTALL
Share Score
PRO TIP
You can share score screenshot by doing a long press on the live screen.
Got it, thanks
2nd Inn (IND)
Session: Open PASS
10 Over 57 runs 79 runs
15 Over 109 runs 111 runs
20 Over 149 runs 142 runs
1st Inn (PAK)
Session: Open PASS
10 Over 49 runs 49 runs
20 Over 99 runs 103 runs
30 Over 157 runs 156 runs
35 Over 184 runs 170 runs
40 Over 193 runs 187 runs
50 Over 216 runs 191 runs
Speech Settings (Accessibility)
NoBroker Rent Pay
Fast and Secure Rent Payments
NOBROKER
Visit Site

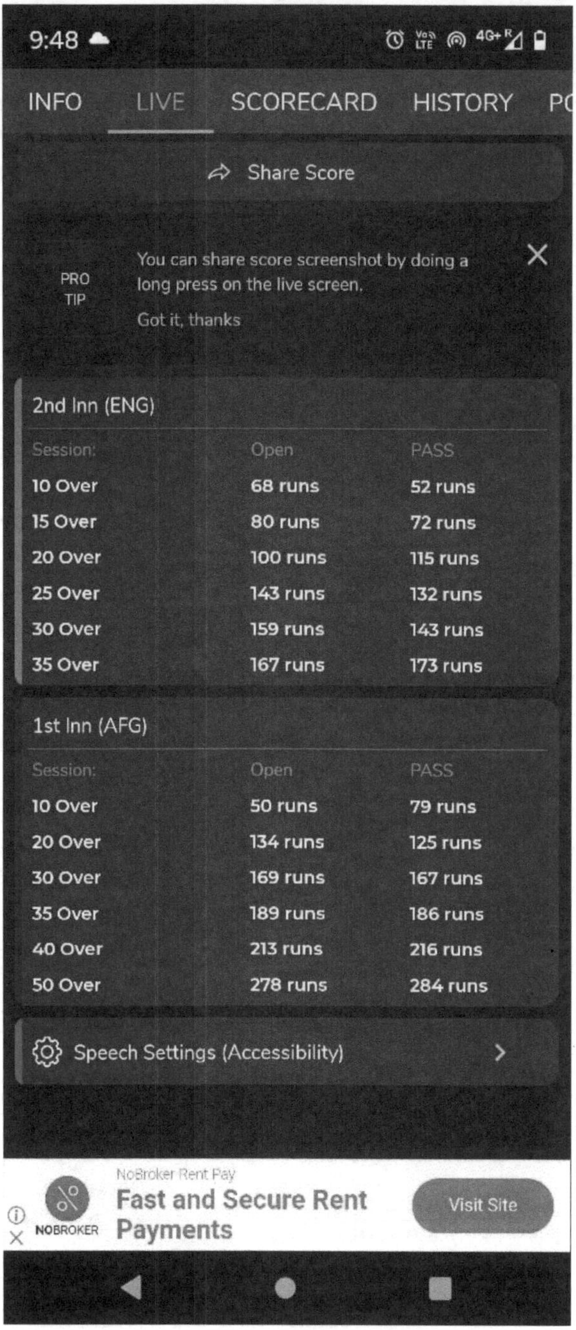
9:48
INFO
LIVE
SCORECARD
HISTORY
Share Score
PRO TIP
You can share score screenshot by doing a long press on the live screen.
Got it, thanks
2nd Inn (ENG)
Session: Open PASS
10 Over 68 runs 52 runs
15 Over 80 runs 72 runs
20 Over 100 runs 115 runs
25 Over 143 runs 132 runs
30 Over 159 runs 143 runs
35 Over 167 runs 173 runs
1st Inn (AFG)
Session: Open PASS
10 Over 50 runs 79 runs
20 Over 134 runs 125 runs
30 Over 169 runs 167 runs
35 Over 189 runs 186 runs
40 Over 213 runs 216 runs
50 Over 278 runs 284 runs
Speech Settings (Accessibility)
NoBroker Rent Pay
Fast and Secure Rent Payments
NOBROKER
Visit Site

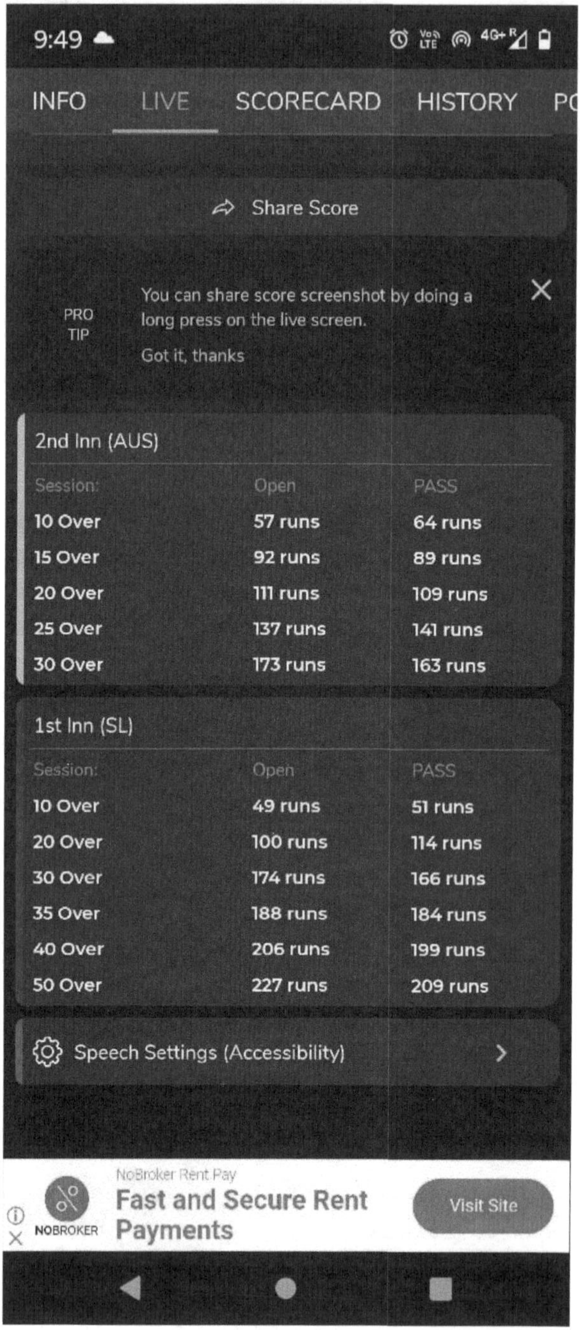
9:49
INFO
LIVE
SCORECARD
HISTORY
Share Score
PRO TIP
You can share score screenshot by doing a long press on the live screen.
Got it, thanks
2nd Inn (AUS)
Session: Open PASS
10 Over 57 runs 64 runs
15 Over 92 runs 89 runs
20 Over 111 runs 109 runs
25 Over 137 runs 141 runs
30 Over 173 runs 163 runs
1st Inn (SL)
Session: Open PASS
10 Over 49 runs 51 runs
20 Over 100 runs 114 runs
30 Over 174 runs 166 runs
35 Over 188 runs 184 runs
40 Over 206 runs 199 runs
50 Over 227 runs 209 runs
Speech Settings (Accessibility)
NoBroker Rent Pay
Fast and Secure Rent Payments
NOBROKER
Visit Site

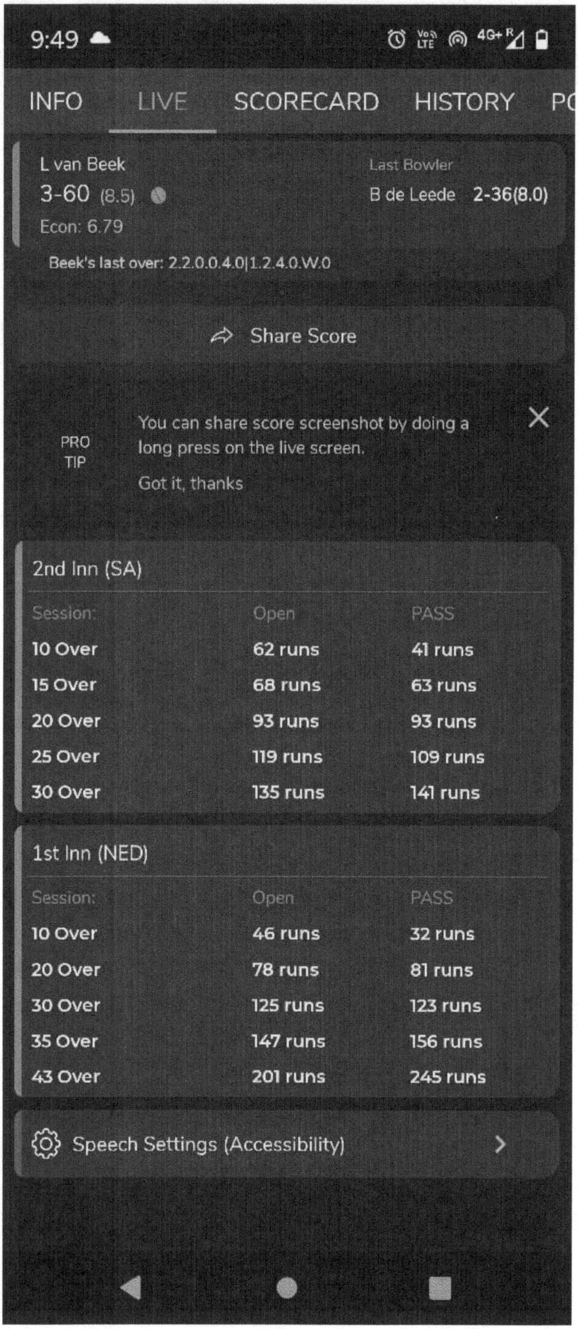
9:49
INFO
LIVE
SCORECARD
HISTORY
L van Beek
3-60 (8.5)
Econ: 6.79
Last Bowler
B de Leede 2-36(8.0)
Beek's last over: 2.2.0.0.4.0|1.2.4.0.W.0
Share Score
PRO TIP
You can share score screenshot by doing a long press on the live screen.
Got it, thanks
2nd Inn (SA)
Session: Open PASS
10 Over 62 runs 41 runs
15 Over 68 runs 63 runs
20 Over 93 runs 93 runs
25 Over 119 runs 109 runs
30 Over 135 runs 141 runs
1st Inn (NED)
Session: Open PASS
10 Over 46 runs 32 runs
20 Over 78 runs 81 runs
30 Over 125 runs 123 runs
35 Over 147 runs 156 runs
43 Over 201 runs 245 runs
Speech Settings (Accessibility)

9:49
INFO
LIVE
SCORECARD
HISTORY
Share Score
PRO TIP
You can share score screenshot by doing a long press on the live screen.
Got it, thanks
2nd Inn (AFG)
Session: Open PASS
10 Over 48 runs 28 runs
15 Over 50 runs 48 runs
20 Over 71 runs 68 runs
25 Over 93 runs 94 runs
30 Over 126 runs 121 runs
35 Over 147 runs 139 runs
1st Inn (NZ)
Session: Open PASS
10 Over 48 runs 43 runs
20 Over 94 runs 109 runs
30 Over 167 runs 138 runs
35 Over 166 runs 163 runs
40 Over 193 runs 185 runs
50 Over 267 runs 288 runs
Speech Settings (Accessibility)
50% + 5%
MEGA XTRAA EVERYTIME
No GST/ No Taxes
PLAY NOW
SPECIAL ID
TRUSTED | SECURE | SAFE

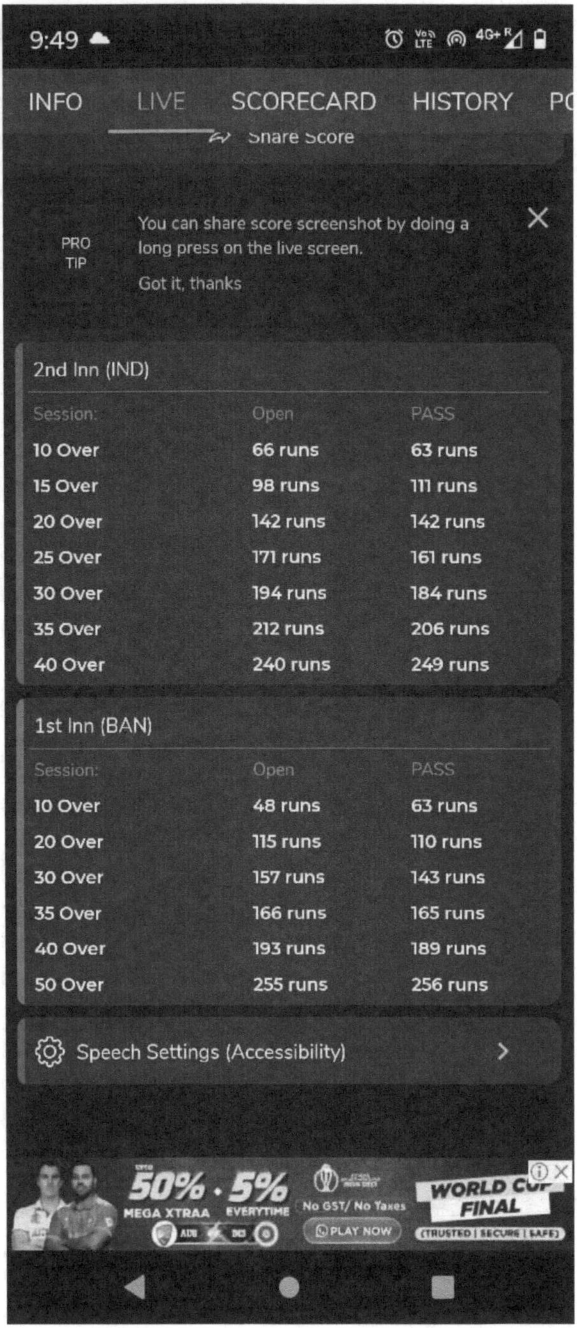
9:49
INFO
LIVE
SCORECARD
HISTORY
Share Score
PRO TIP
You can share score screenshot by doing a long press on the live screen.
Got it, thanks
2nd Inn (IND)
Session: Open PASS
10 Over 66 runs 63 runs
15 Over 98 runs 111 runs
20 Over 142 runs 142 runs
25 Over 171 runs 161 runs
30 Over 194 runs 184 runs
35 Over 212 runs 206 runs
40 Over 240 runs 249 runs
1st Inn (BAN)
Session: Open PASS
10 Over 48 runs 63 runs
20 Over 115 runs 110 runs
30 Over 157 runs 143 runs
35 Over 166 runs 165 runs
40 Over 193 runs 189 runs
50 Over 255 runs 256 runs
Speech Settings (Accessibility)
50% · 5%
MEGA XTRAA
EVERYTIME
No GST/ No Taxes
PLAY NOW
WORLD CUP
FINAL

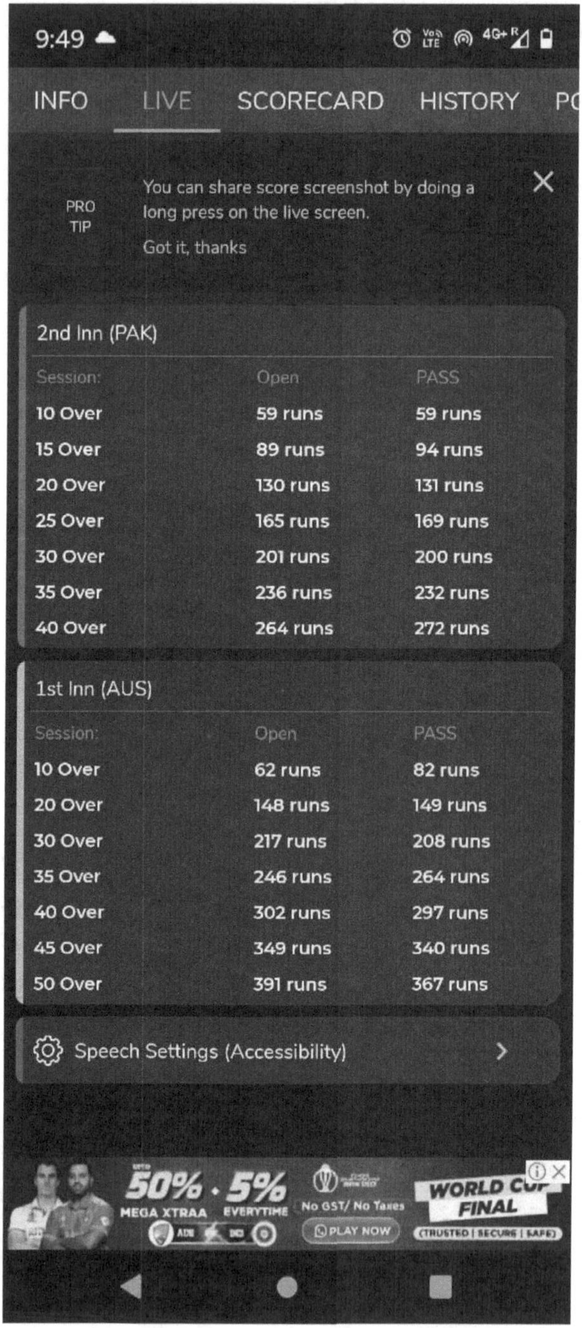

9:49

INFO LIVE SCORECARD HISTORY P

PRO TIP

You can share score screenshot by doing a long press on the live screen.

Got it, thanks

2nd Inn (PAK)

Session:	Open	PASS
10 Over	59 runs	59 runs
15 Over	89 runs	94 runs
20 Over	130 runs	131 runs
25 Over	165 runs	169 runs
30 Over	201 runs	200 runs
35 Over	236 runs	232 runs
40 Over	264 runs	272 runs

1st Inn (AUS)

Session:	Open	PASS
10 Over	62 runs	82 runs
20 Over	148 runs	149 runs
30 Over	217 runs	208 runs
35 Over	246 runs	264 runs
40 Over	302 runs	297 runs
45 Over	349 runs	340 runs
50 Over	391 runs	367 runs

Speech Settings (Accessibility)

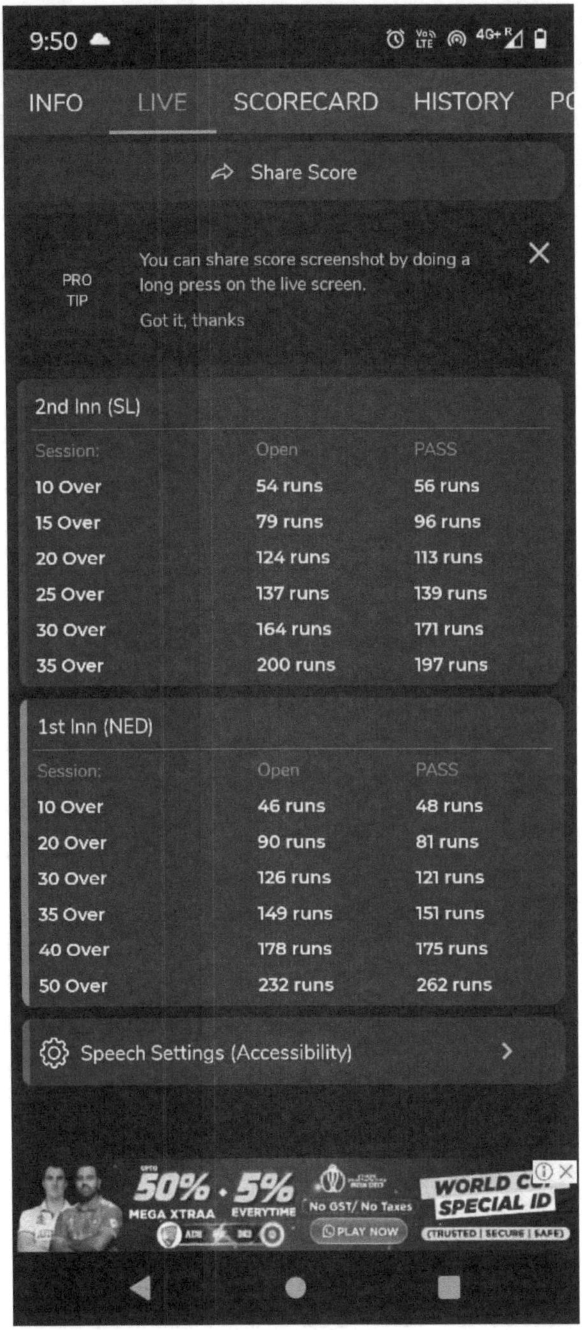
9:50
INFO
LIVE
SCORECARD
HISTORY
Share Score
PRO TIP
You can share score screenshot by doing a long press on the live screen.
Got it, thanks
2nd Inn (SL)
Session: Open PASS
10 Over 54 runs 56 runs
15 Over 79 runs 96 runs
20 Over 124 runs 113 runs
25 Over 137 runs 139 runs
30 Over 164 runs 171 runs
35 Over 200 runs 197 runs
1st Inn (NED)
Session: Open PASS
10 Over 46 runs 48 runs
20 Over 90 runs 81 runs
30 Over 126 runs 121 runs
35 Over 149 runs 151 runs
40 Over 178 runs 175 runs
50 Over 232 runs 262 runs
Speech Settings (Accessibility)
50% · 5%
MEGA XTRAA
EVERYTIME
No GST/ No Taxes
PLAY NOW
SPECIAL ID

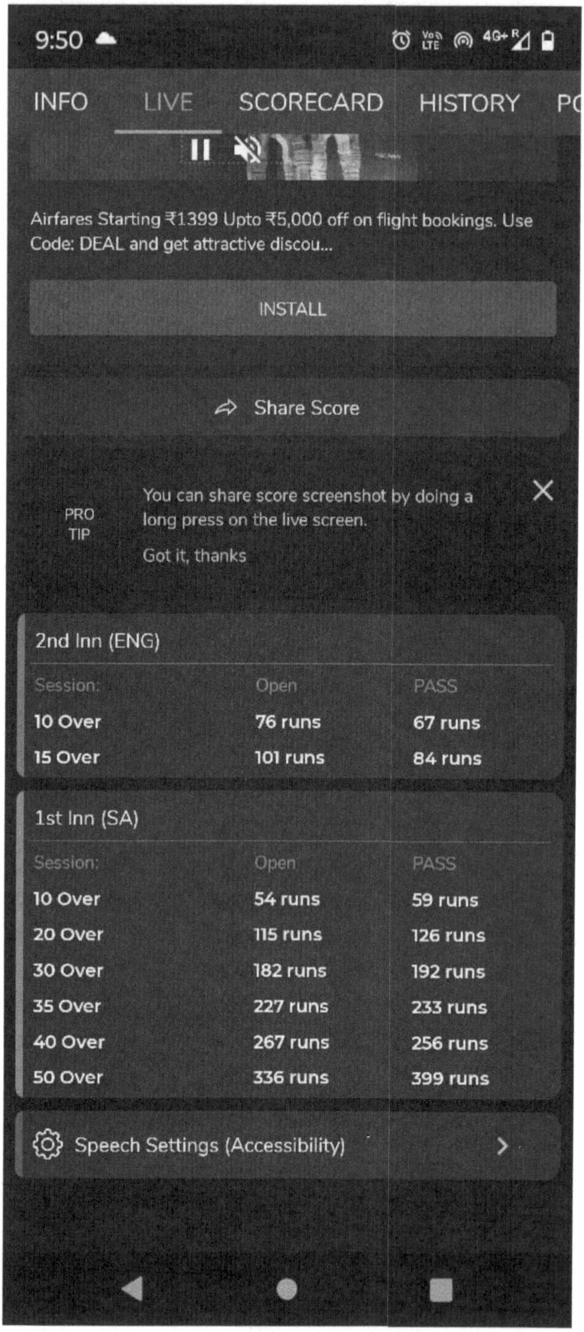
9:50
INFO
LIVE
SCORECARD
HISTORY
Airfares Starting ₹1399 Upto ₹5,000 off on flight bookings. Use Code: DEAL and get attractive discou...
INSTALL
Share Score
PRO TIP
You can share score screenshot by doing a long press on the live screen.
Got it, thanks
2nd Inn (ENG)
Session: Open PASS
10 Over 76 runs 67 runs
15 Over 101 runs 84 runs
1st Inn (SA)
Session: Open PASS
10 Over 54 runs 59 runs
20 Over 115 runs 126 runs
30 Over 182 runs 192 runs
35 Over 227 runs 233 runs
40 Over 267 runs 256 runs
50 Over 336 runs 399 runs
Speech Settings (Accessibility)

2nd Inn (IND)

Session:	Open	PASS
10 Over	58 runs	63 runs
15 Over	90 runs	91 runs
20 Over	121 runs	121 runs
25 Over	147 runs	140 runs
30 Over	166 runs	168 runs
35 Over	196 runs	192 runs
40 Over	219 runs	225 runs

1st Inn (NZ)

Session:	Open	PASS
10 Over	50 runs	34 runs
20 Over	84 runs	91 runs
30 Over	148 runs	147 runs
35 Over	180 runs	187 runs
40 Over	217 runs	219 runs
50 Over	299 runs	273 runs

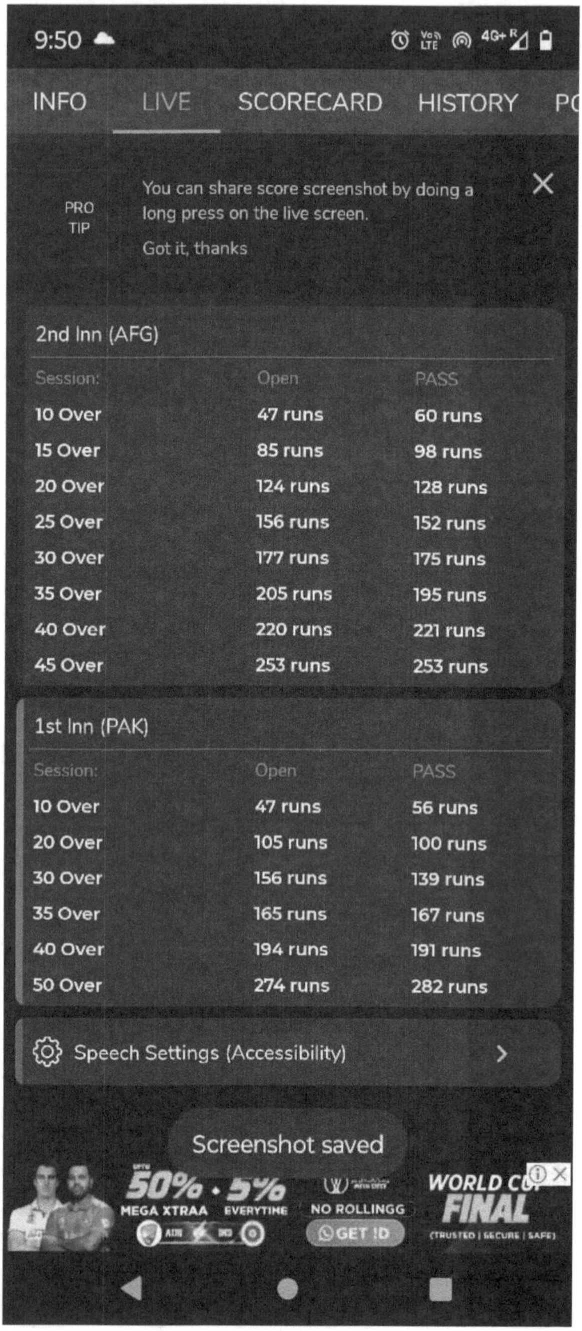
9:50
INFO
LIVE
SCORECARD
HISTORY
PRO TIP
You can share score screenshot by doing a long press on the live screen.
Got it, thanks
2nd Inn (AFG)
Session: Open PASS
10 Over 47 runs 60 runs
15 Over 85 runs 98 runs
20 Over 124 runs 128 runs
25 Over 156 runs 152 runs
30 Over 177 runs 175 runs
35 Over 205 runs 195 runs
40 Over 220 runs 221 runs
45 Over 253 runs 253 runs
1st Inn (PAK)
Session: Open PASS
10 Over 47 runs 56 runs
20 Over 105 runs 100 runs
30 Over 156 runs 139 runs
35 Over 165 runs 167 runs
40 Over 194 runs 191 runs
50 Over 274 runs 282 runs
Speech Settings (Accessibility)
Screenshot saved
50% · 5%
MEGA XTRAA
EVERYTIME
NO ROLLINGG
GET ID
FINAL
(TRUSTED | SECURE | SAFE)

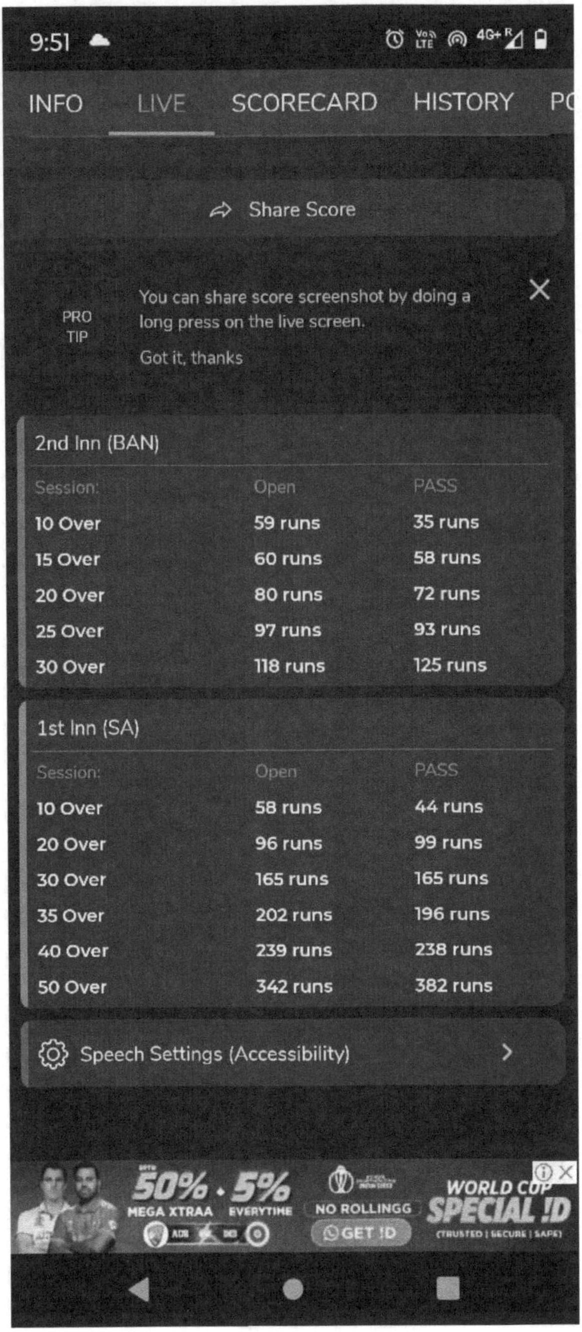
9:51
INFO
LIVE
SCORECARD
HISTORY
Share Score
PRO TIP
You can share score screenshot by doing a long press on the live screen.
Got it, thanks
2nd Inn (BAN)
Session: Open PASS
10 Over 59 runs 35 runs
15 Over 60 runs 58 runs
20 Over 80 runs 72 runs
25 Over 97 runs 93 runs
30 Over 118 runs 125 runs
1st Inn (SA)
Session: Open PASS
10 Over 58 runs 44 runs
20 Over 96 runs 99 runs
30 Over 165 runs 165 runs
35 Over 202 runs 196 runs
40 Over 239 runs 238 runs
50 Over 342 runs 382 runs
Speech Settings (Accessibility)
50% · 5%
MEGA XTRAA
EVERYTIME
NO ROLLINGG
GET ID
WORLD CUP
SPECIAL ID
(TRUSTED | SECURE | SAFE)

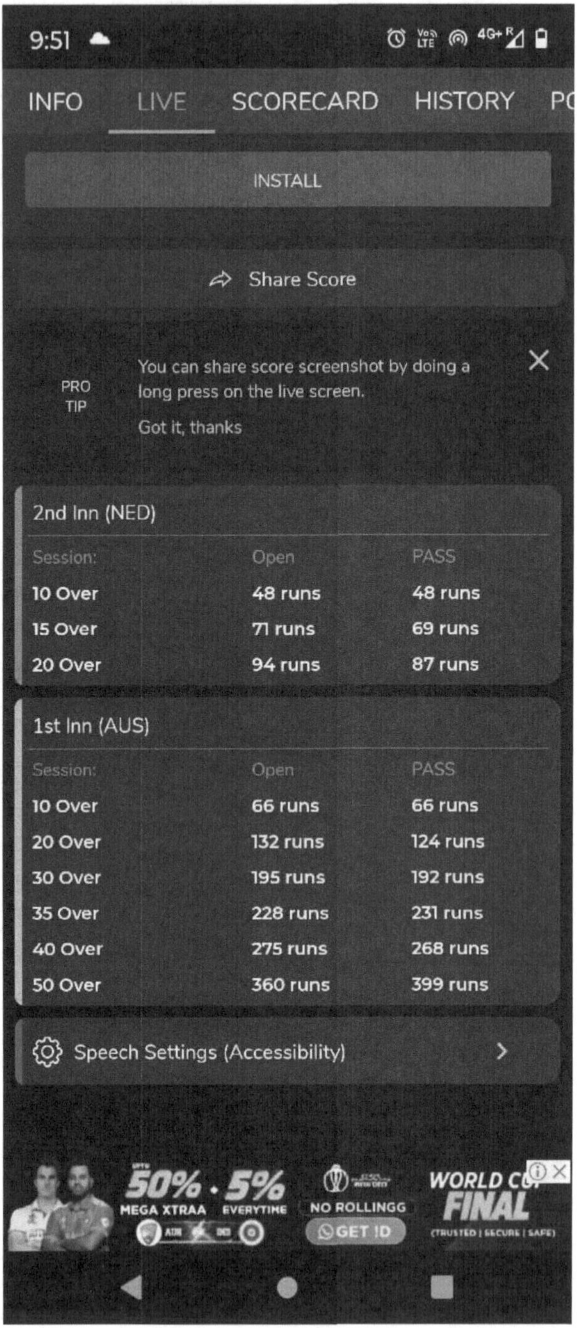
9:51
INFO
LIVE
SCORECARD
HISTORY
INSTALL
Share Score
PRO TIP
You can share score screenshot by doing a long press on the live screen.
Got it, thanks
2nd Inn (NED)
Session: Open PASS
10 Over 48 runs 48 runs
15 Over 71 runs 69 runs
20 Over 94 runs 87 runs
1st Inn (AUS)
Session: Open PASS
10 Over 66 runs 66 runs
20 Over 132 runs 124 runs
30 Over 195 runs 192 runs
35 Over 228 runs 231 runs
40 Over 275 runs 268 runs
50 Over 360 runs 399 runs
Speech Settings (Accessibility)
50% · 5%
MEGA XTRAA
EVERYTIME
NO ROLLINGG
GET ID
FINAL

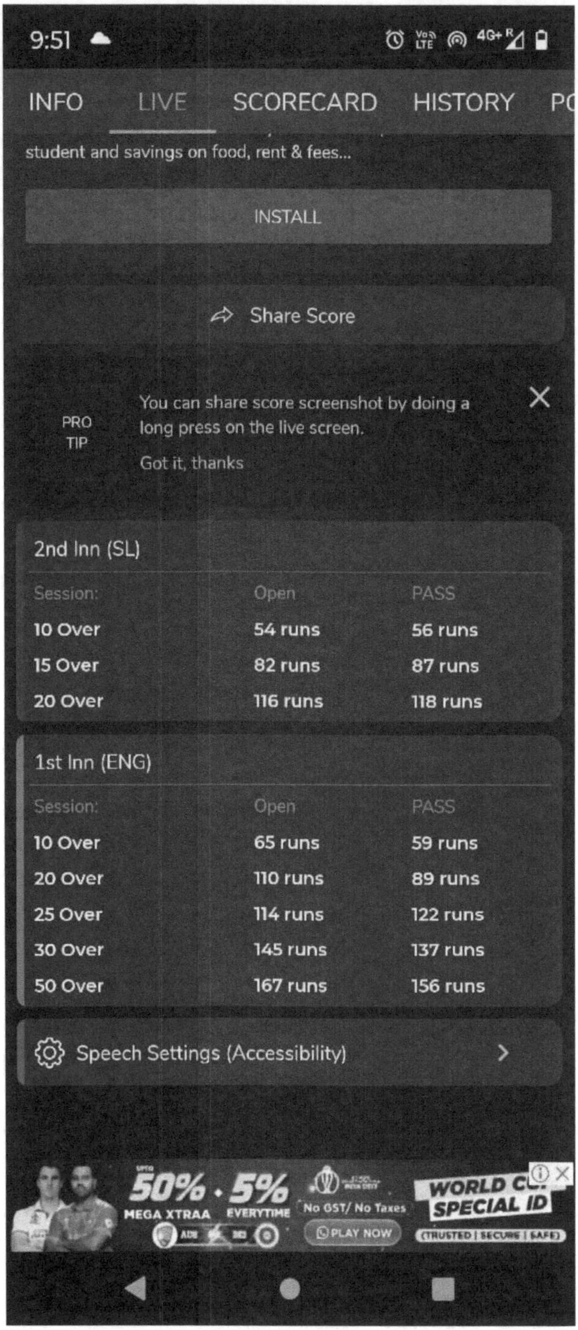
9:51
INFO
LIVE
SCORECARD
HISTORY
student and savings on food, rent & fees...
INSTALL
Share Score
PRO TIP
You can share score screenshot by doing a long press on the live screen.
Got it, thanks
2nd Inn (SL)
Session: Open PASS
10 Over 54 runs 56 runs
15 Over 82 runs 87 runs
20 Over 116 runs 118 runs
1st Inn (ENG)
Session: Open PASS
10 Over 65 runs 59 runs
20 Over 110 runs 89 runs
25 Over 114 runs 122 runs
30 Over 145 runs 137 runs
50 Over 167 runs 156 runs
Speech Settings (Accessibility)
50% · 5%
MEGA XTRAA EVERYTIME
No GST/ No Taxes
PLAY NOW
SPECIAL ID
(TRUSTED | SECURE | SAFE)

9:51
INFO
LIVE
SCORECARD
HISTORY
Share Score
PRO TIP
You can share score screenshot by doing a long press on the live screen.
Got it, thanks
2nd Inn (SA)
Session: Open PASS
10 Over 53 runs 67 runs
15 Over 91 runs 107 runs
20 Over 139 runs 125 runs
25 Over 153 runs 154 runs
30 Over 181 runs 191 runs
35 Over 223 runs 214 runs
40 Over 245 runs 249 runs
1st Inn (PAK)
Session: Open PASS
10 Over 48 runs 58 runs
20 Over 108 runs 102 runs
30 Over 155 runs 151 runs
35 Over 178 runs 189 runs
40 Over 224 runs 225 runs
50 Over 294 runs 270 runs
Speech Settings (Accessibility)
50% · 5%
MEGA XTRAA
EVERYTIME
No GST/ No Taxes
PLAY NOW
FINAL

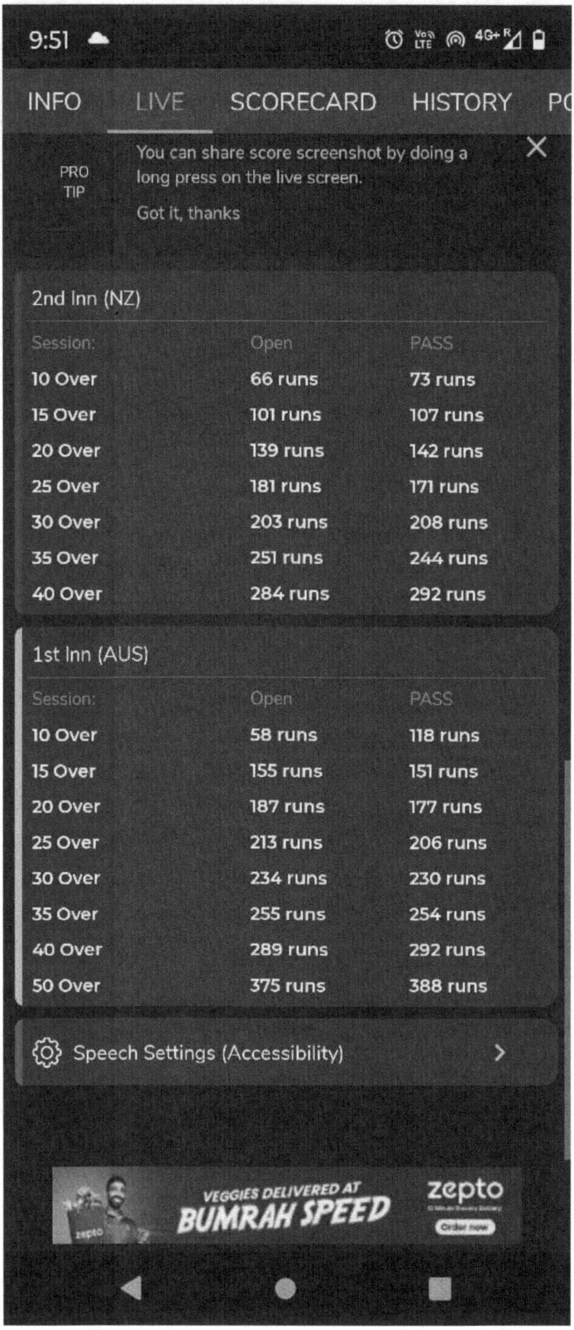
9:51

INFO LIVE SCORECARD HISTORY PC

PRO TIP

You can share score screenshot by doing a long press on the live screen.

Got it, thanks

2nd Inn (NZ)

Session:	Open	PASS
10 Over	66 runs	73 runs
15 Over	101 runs	107 runs
20 Over	139 runs	142 runs
25 Over	181 runs	171 runs
30 Over	203 runs	208 runs
35 Over	251 runs	244 runs
40 Over	284 runs	292 runs

1st Inn (AUS)

Session:	Open	PASS
10 Over	58 runs	118 runs
15 Over	155 runs	151 runs
20 Over	187 runs	177 runs
25 Over	213 runs	206 runs
30 Over	234 runs	230 runs
35 Over	255 runs	254 runs
40 Over	289 runs	292 runs
50 Over	375 runs	388 runs

Speech Settings (Accessibility)

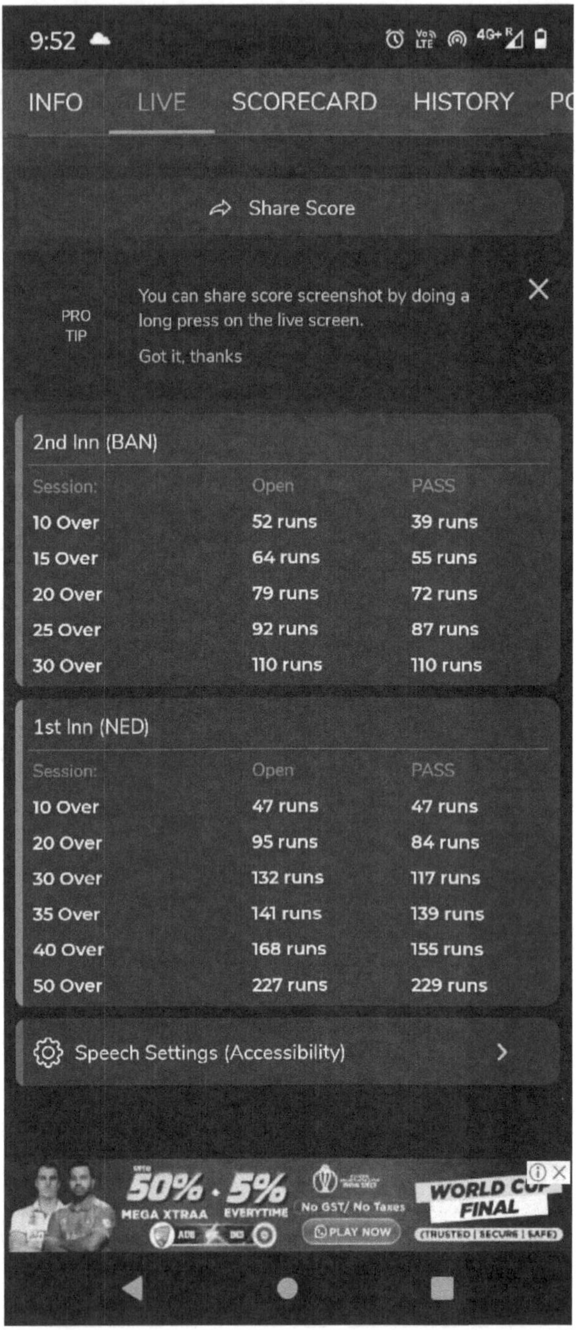
9:52
INFO
LIVE
SCORECARD
HISTORY
Share Score
PRO TIP
You can share score screenshot by doing a long press on the live screen.
Got it, thanks
2nd Inn (BAN)
Session: Open PASS
10 Over 52 runs 39 runs
15 Over 64 runs 55 runs
20 Over 79 runs 72 runs
25 Over 92 runs 87 runs
30 Over 110 runs 110 runs
1st Inn (NED)
Session: Open PASS
10 Over 47 runs 47 runs
20 Over 95 runs 84 runs
30 Over 132 runs 117 runs
35 Over 141 runs 139 runs
40 Over 168 runs 155 runs
50 Over 227 runs 229 runs
Speech Settings (Accessibility)
50% MEGA XTRAA
5% EVERYTIME
No GST/ No Taxes
PLAY NOW
FINAL

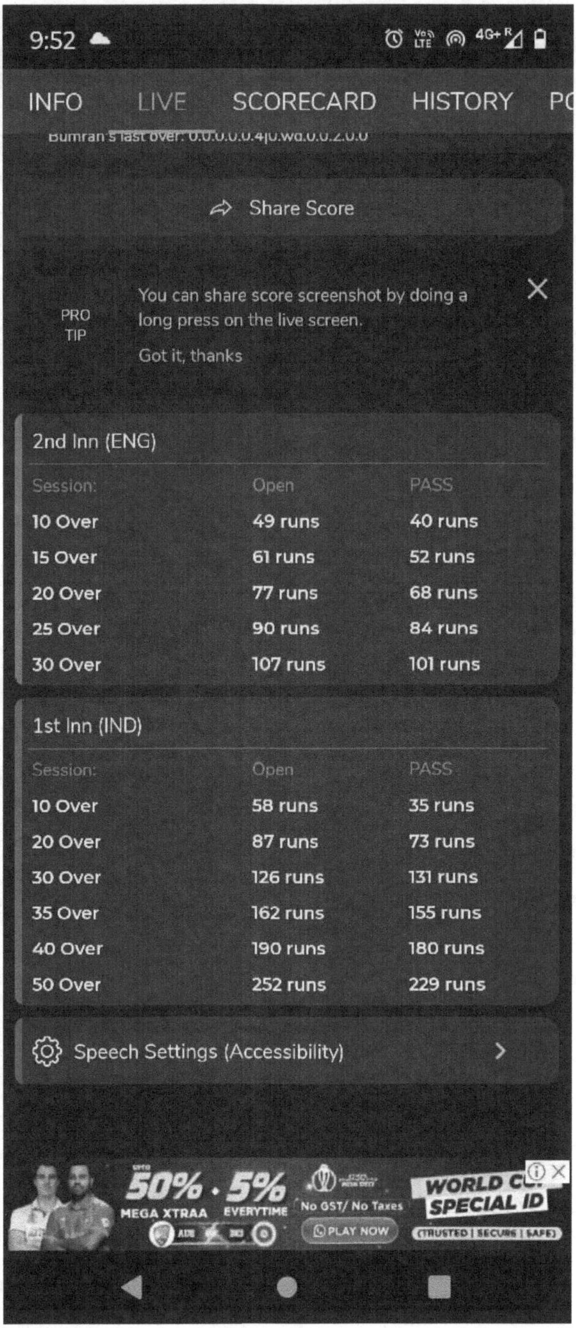
9:52
INFO
LIVE
SCORECARD
HISTORY
Share Score
PRO TIP
You can share score screenshot by doing a long press on the live screen.
Got it, thanks
2nd Inn (ENG)
Session: Open PASS
10 Over 49 runs 40 runs
15 Over 61 runs 52 runs
20 Over 77 runs 68 runs
25 Over 90 runs 84 runs
30 Over 107 runs 101 runs
1st Inn (IND)
Session: Open PASS
10 Over 58 runs 35 runs
20 Over 87 runs 73 runs
30 Over 126 runs 131 runs
35 Over 162 runs 155 runs
40 Over 190 runs 180 runs
50 Over 252 runs 229 runs
Speech Settings (Accessibility)
50% · 5%
MEGA XTRAA
EVERYTIME
No GST/ No Taxes
PLAY NOW
SPECIAL ID
(TRUSTED | SECURE | SAFE)

9:52
INFO
LIVE
SCORECARD
HISTORY
Share Score
PRO TIP
You can share score screenshot by doing a long press on the live screen.
Got it, thanks
2nd Inn (AFG)
Session: Open PASS
10 Over 48 runs 50 runs
15 Over 73 runs 67 runs
20 Over 91 runs 87 runs
25 Over 112 runs 119 runs
30 Over 145 runs 139 runs
35 Over 163 runs 166 runs
40 Over 193 runs 201 runs
1st Inn (SL)
Session: Open PASS
10 Over 52 runs 41 runs
20 Over 94 runs 87 runs
30 Over 139 runs 144 runs
35 Over 168 runs 166 runs
40 Over 196 runs 185 runs
50 Over 230 runs 241 runs
Speech Settings (Accessibility)
Junglee Rummy
4.2 FREE
INSTALL

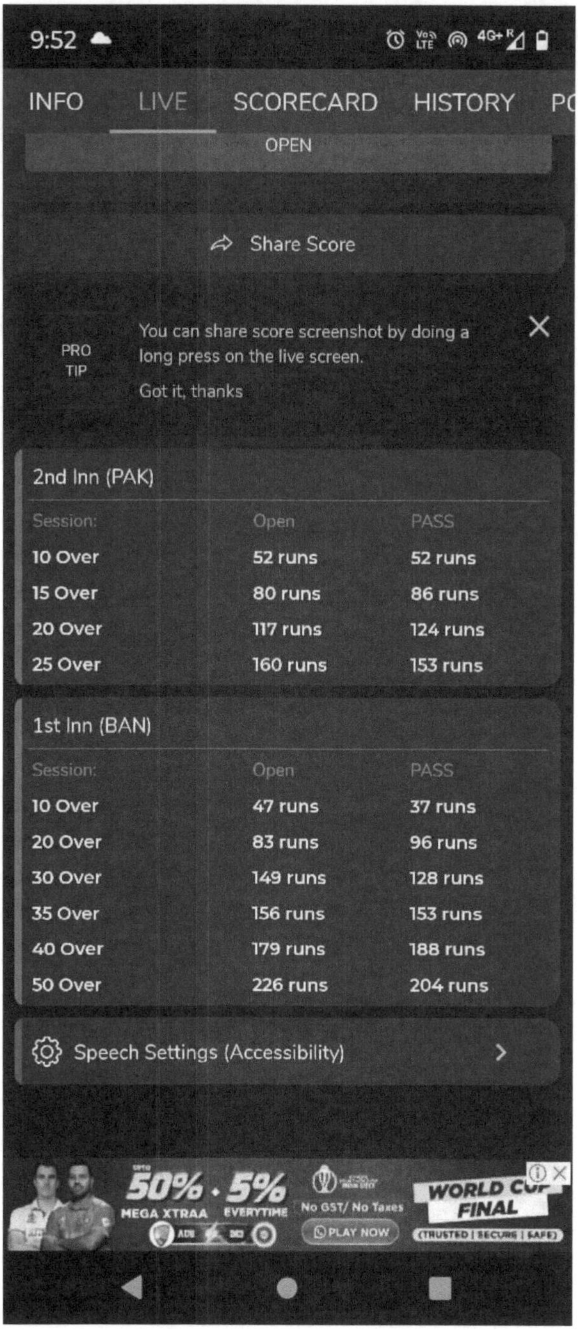
9:52
INFO
LIVE
SCORECARD
HISTORY
OPEN
Share Score
PRO TIP
You can share score screenshot by doing a long press on the live screen.
Got it, thanks
2nd Inn (PAK)
Session: Open PASS
10 Over 52 runs 52 runs
15 Over 80 runs 86 runs
20 Over 117 runs 124 runs
25 Over 160 runs 153 runs
1st Inn (BAN)
Session: Open PASS
10 Over 47 runs 37 runs
20 Over 83 runs 96 runs
30 Over 149 runs 128 runs
35 Over 156 runs 153 runs
40 Over 179 runs 188 runs
50 Over 226 runs 204 runs
Speech Settings (Accessibility)
50% · 5%
MEGA XTRAA EVERYTIME
No GST/ No Taxes
PLAY NOW
FINAL
(TRUSTED | SECURE | SAFE)

9:52
INFO
LIVE
SCORECARD
HISTORY
Share Score
PRO TIP
You can share score screenshot by doing a long press on the live screen.
Got it, thanks
2nd Inn (NZ)
Session: Open PASS
10 Over 60 runs 51 runs
15 Over 78 runs 67 runs
20 Over 95 runs 91 runs
25 Over 112 runs 109 runs
1st Inn (SA)
Session: Open PASS
10 Over 53 runs 43 runs
20 Over 96 runs 94 runs
30 Over 158 runs 155 runs
35 Over 193 runs 194 runs
40 Over 236 runs 238 runs
45 Over 284 runs 290 runs
50 Over 356 runs 357 runs
Speech Settings (Accessibility)
50% · 5%
MEGA XTRAA
EVERYTIME
No GST/ No Taxes
PLAY NOW
SPECIAL ID

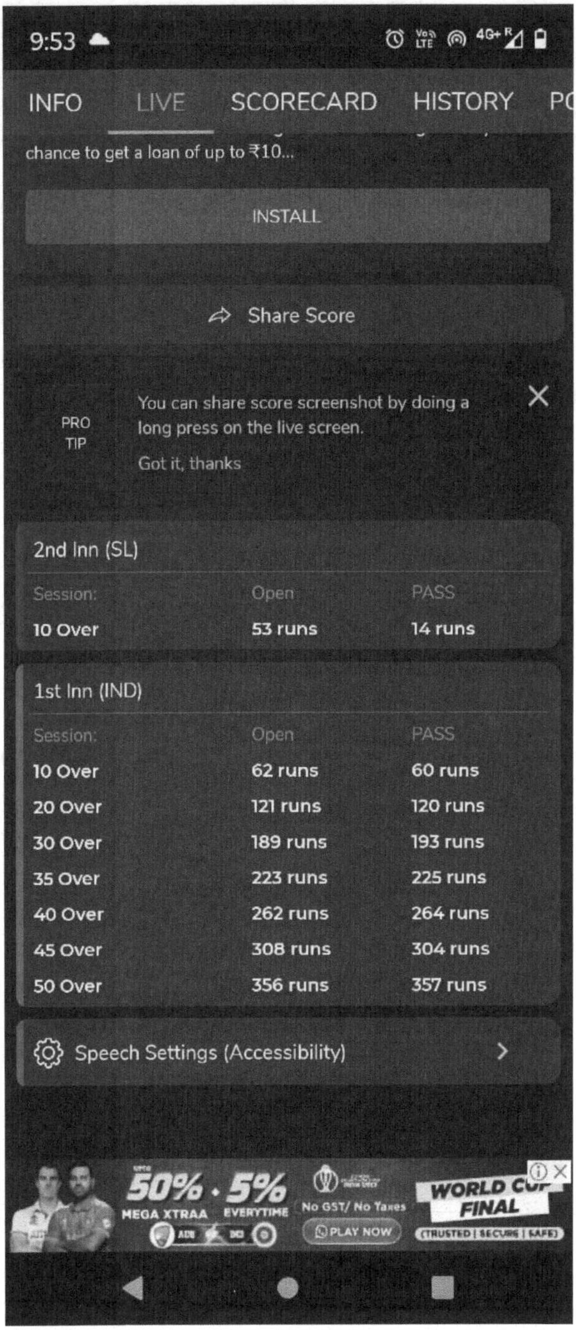
9:53
INFO
LIVE
SCORECARD
HISTORY
chance to get a loan of up to ₹10...
INSTALL
Share Score
PRO TIP
You can share score screenshot by doing a long press on the live screen.
Got it, thanks
2nd Inn (SL)
Session: Open PASS
10 Over 53 runs 14 runs
1st Inn (IND)
Session: Open PASS
10 Over 62 runs 60 runs
20 Over 121 runs 120 runs
30 Over 189 runs 193 runs
35 Over 223 runs 225 runs
40 Over 262 runs 264 runs
45 Over 308 runs 304 runs
50 Over 356 runs 357 runs
Speech Settings (Accessibility)
50% · 5%
MEGA XTRAA EVERYTIME
No GST/ No Taxes
PLAY NOW
FINAL
TRUSTED | SECURE | SAFE

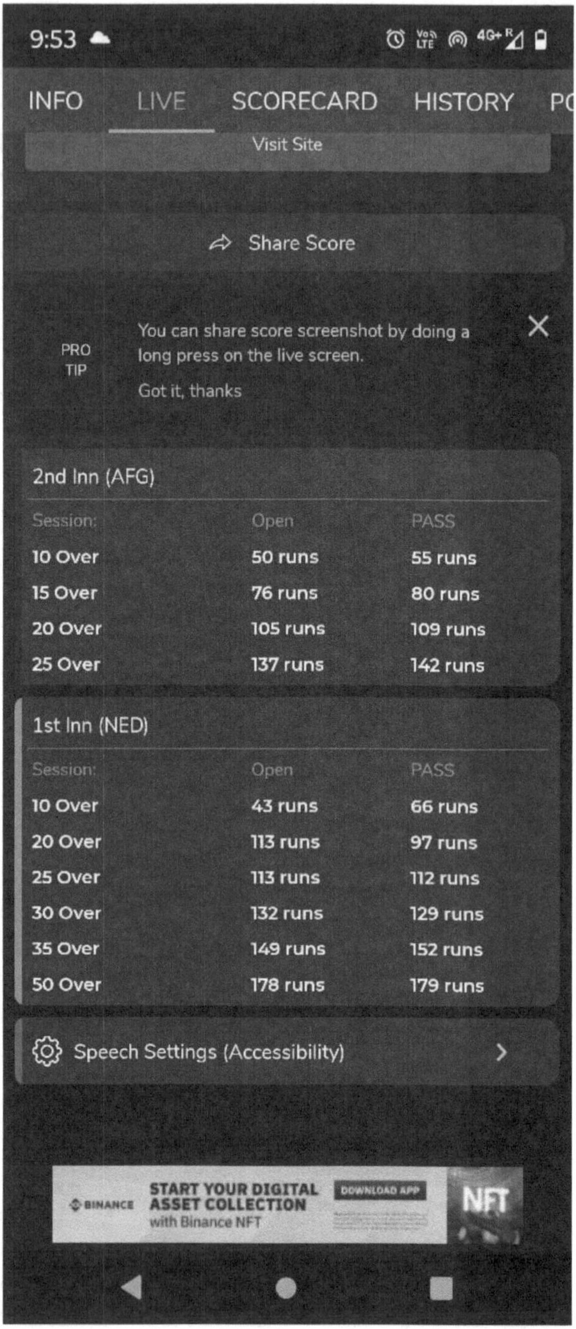
9:53
INFO
LIVE
SCORECARD
HISTORY
Visit Site
Share Score
PRO TIP
You can share score screenshot by doing a long press on the live screen.
Got it, thanks
2nd Inn (AFG)
Session: Open PASS
10 Over 50 runs 55 runs
15 Over 76 runs 80 runs
20 Over 105 runs 109 runs
25 Over 137 runs 142 runs
1st Inn (NED)
Session: Open PASS
10 Over 43 runs 66 runs
20 Over 113 runs 97 runs
25 Over 113 runs 112 runs
30 Over 132 runs 129 runs
35 Over 149 runs 152 runs
50 Over 178 runs 179 runs
Speech Settings (Accessibility)
BINANCE
START YOUR DIGITAL ASSET COLLECTION
with Binance NFT
DOWNLOAD APP
NFT

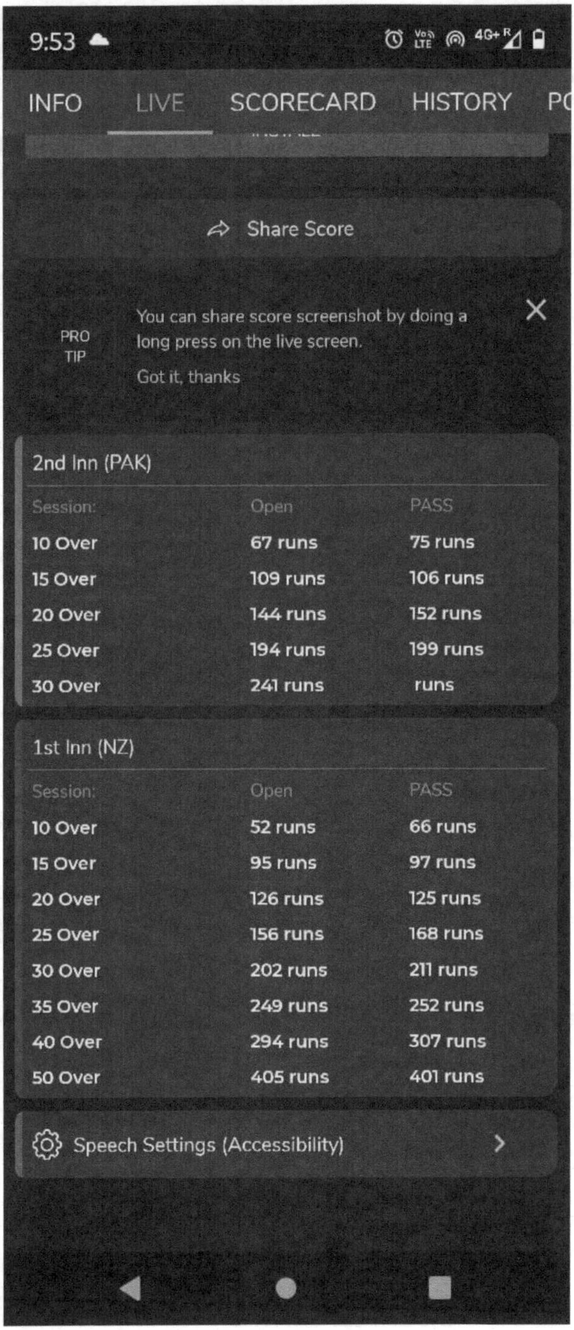
9:53
INFO
LIVE
SCORECARD
HISTORY
Share Score
PRO TIP
You can share score screenshot by doing a long press on the live screen.
Got it, thanks
2nd Inn (PAK)
Session: Open PASS
10 Over 67 runs 75 runs
15 Over 109 runs 106 runs
20 Over 144 runs 152 runs
25 Over 194 runs 199 runs
30 Over 241 runs runs
1st Inn (NZ)
Session: Open PASS
10 Over 52 runs 66 runs
15 Over 95 runs 97 runs
20 Over 126 runs 125 runs
25 Over 156 runs 168 runs
30 Over 202 runs 211 runs
35 Over 249 runs 252 runs
40 Over 294 runs 307 runs
50 Over 405 runs 401 runs
Speech Settings (Accessibility)

9:53
INFO
LIVE
SCORECARD
HISTORY
Share Score
PRO TIP
You can share score screenshot by doing a long press on the live screen.
Got it, thanks
2nd Inn (ENG)
Session: Open PASS
10 Over 55 runs 38 runs
15 Over 65 runs 58 runs
20 Over 87 runs 82 runs
25 Over 111 runs 106 runs
30 Over 129 runs 128 runs
35 Over 158 runs 169 runs
1st Inn (AUS)
Session: Open PASS
10 Over 66 runs 48 runs
20 Over 100 runs 101 runs
30 Over 158 runs 153 runs
35 Over 181 runs 190 runs
40 Over 219 runs 220 runs
50 Over 300 runs 286 runs
Speech Settings (Accessibility)
Junglee Rummy
4.2 FREE
INSTALL

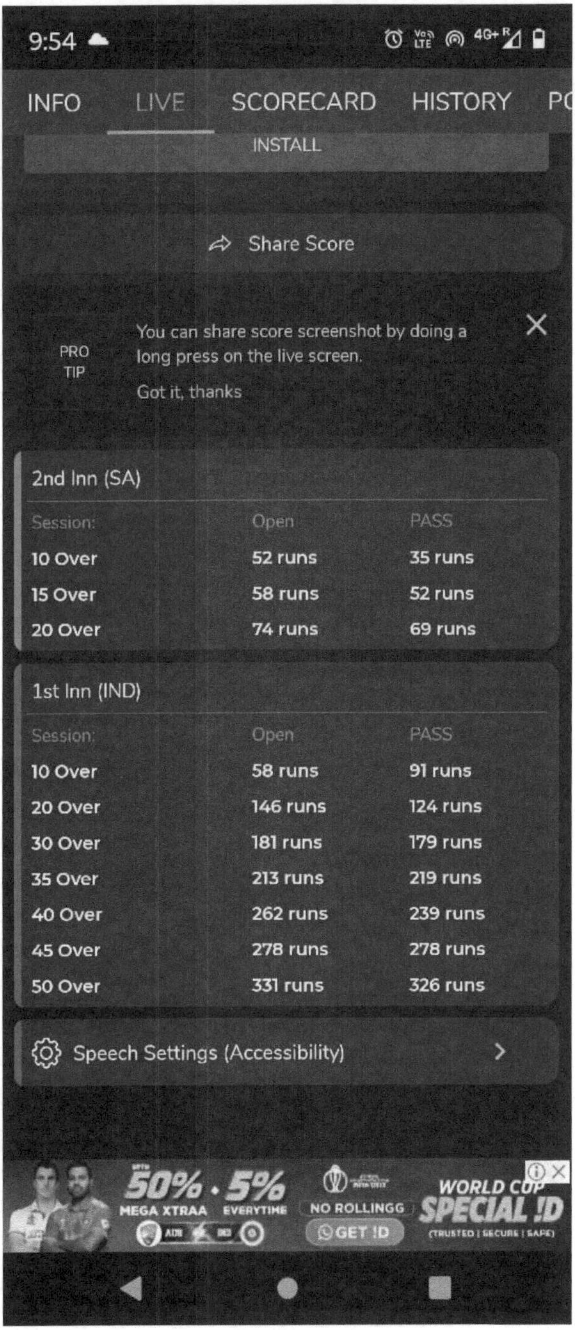
9:54
INFO
LIVE
SCORECARD
HISTORY
INSTALL
Share Score
PRO TIP
You can share score screenshot by doing a long press on the live screen.
Got it, thanks
2nd Inn (SA)
Session: Open PASS
10 Over 52 runs 35 runs
15 Over 58 runs 52 runs
20 Over 74 runs 69 runs
1st Inn (IND)
Session: Open PASS
10 Over 58 runs 91 runs
20 Over 146 runs 124 runs
30 Over 181 runs 179 runs
35 Over 213 runs 219 runs
40 Over 262 runs 239 runs
45 Over 278 runs 278 runs
50 Over 331 runs 326 runs
Speech Settings (Accessibility)
50% · 5%
MEGA XTRAA
EVERYTIME
NO ROLLINGG
GET ID
WORLD CUP
SPECIAL ID
(TRUSTED | SECURE | SAFE)

9:54
INFO
LIVE
SCORECARD
HISTORY
Share Score
PRO TIP
You can share score screenshot by doing a long press on the live screen.
Got it, thanks
2nd Inn (BAN)
Session: Open PASS
10 Over 50 runs 57 runs
15 Over 82 runs 81 runs
20 Over 107 runs 123 runs
25 Over 161 runs 161 runs
30 Over 194 runs 206 runs
35 Over 243 runs 224 runs
40 Over 253 runs 268 runs
1st Inn (SL)
Session: Open PASS
10 Over 55 runs 52 runs
20 Over 109 runs 113 runs
30 Over 169 runs 162 runs
35 Over 190 runs 196 runs
40 Over 229 runs 223 runs
50 Over 290 runs 279 runs
Speech Settings (Accessibility)
50% · 5%
MEGA XTRAA
EVERYTIME
NO ROLLINGG
GET ID
WORLD CUP
SPECIAL ID
(TRUSTED | SECURE | SAFE)

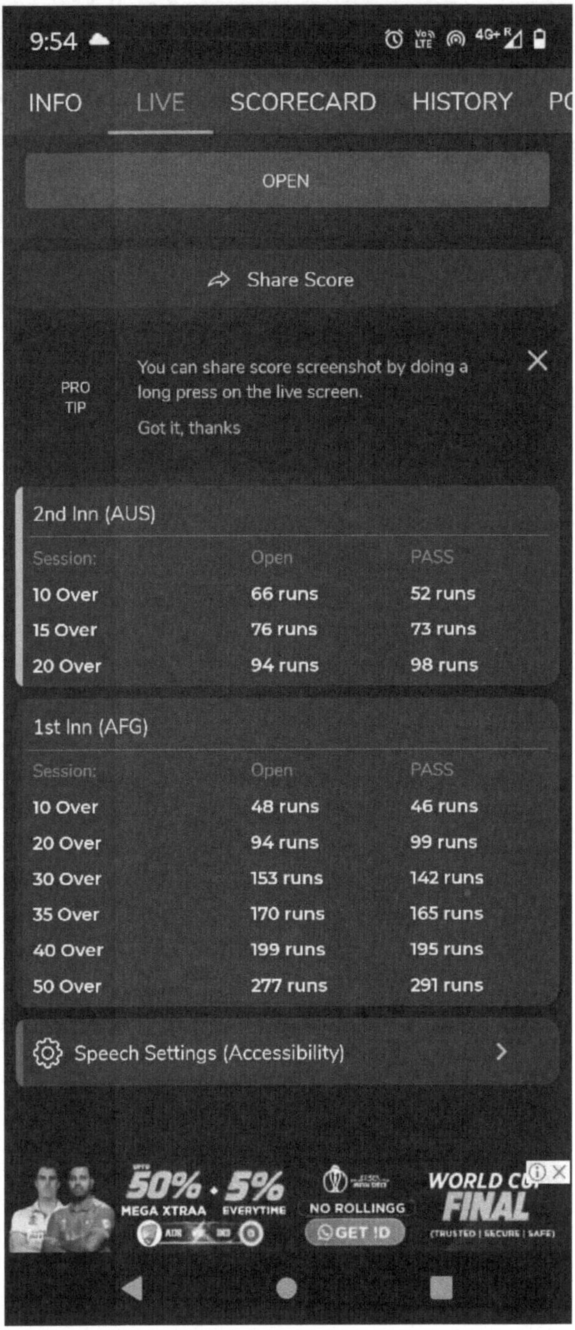
9:54
INFO
LIVE
SCORECARD
HISTORY
OPEN
Share Score
PRO TIP
You can share score screenshot by doing a long press on the live screen.
Got it, thanks
2nd Inn (AUS)
Session: Open PASS
10 Over 66 runs 52 runs
15 Over 76 runs 73 runs
20 Over 94 runs 98 runs
1st Inn (AFG)
Session: Open PASS
10 Over 48 runs 46 runs
20 Over 94 runs 99 runs
30 Over 153 runs 142 runs
35 Over 170 runs 165 runs
40 Over 199 runs 195 runs
50 Over 277 runs 291 runs
Speech Settings (Accessibility)
50% · 5%
MEGA XTRAA
EVERYTIME
NO ROLLINGG
GET ID
FINAL
(TRUSTED | SECURE | SAFE)

9:54
INFO
LIVE
SCORECARD
HISTORY
Share Score
PRO TIP
You can share score screenshot by doing a long press on the live screen.
Got it, thanks
2nd Inn (NED)
Session: Open PASS
10 Over 50 runs 23 runs
15 Over 46 runs 57 runs
20 Over 83 runs 77 runs
25 Over 105 runs 99 runs
30 Over 126 runs 140 runs
35 Over 174 runs 166 runs
1st Inn (ENG)
Session: Open PASS
10 Over 64 runs 70 runs
20 Over 132 runs 132 runs
30 Over 201 runs 178 runs
35 Over 212 runs 191 runs
40 Over 226 runs 215 runs
50 Over 297 runs 339 runs
Speech Settings (Accessibility)
50% · 5%
MEGA XTRAA EVERYTIME
NO ROLLINGG
GET ID
FINAL
(TRUSTED | SECURE | SAFE)

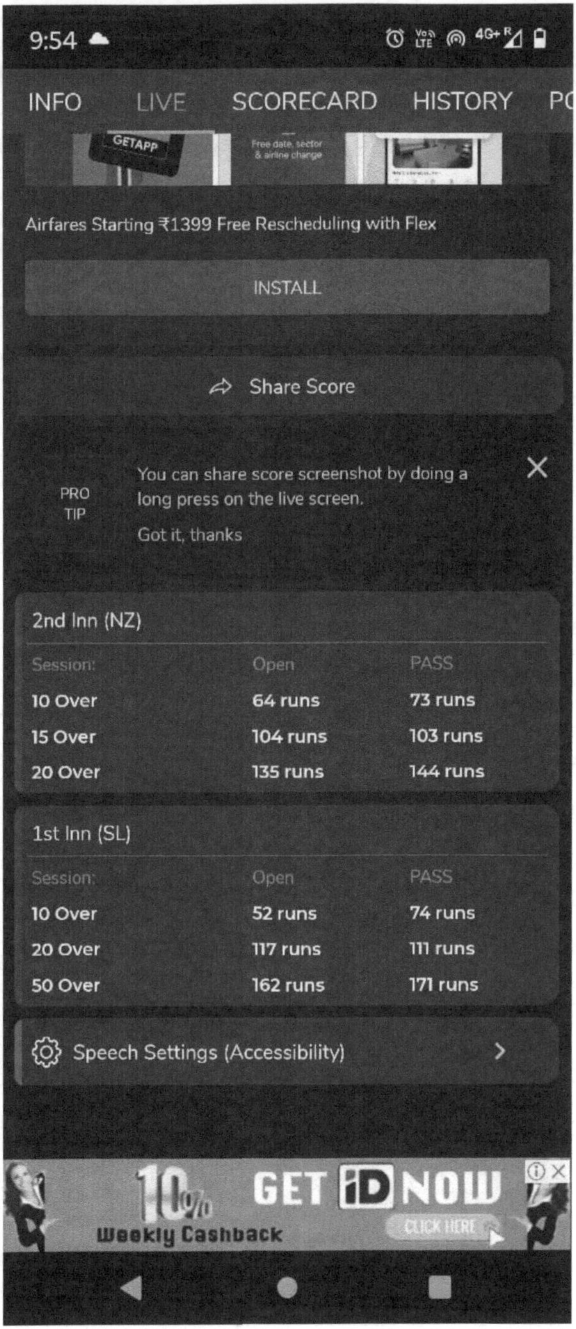
9:54
INFO
LIVE
SCORECARD
HISTORY
GETAPP
Airfares Starting ₹1399 Free Rescheduling with Flex
INSTALL
Share Score
PRO TIP
You can share score screenshot by doing a long press on the live screen.
Got it, thanks
2nd Inn (NZ)
Session: Open PASS
10 Over 64 runs 73 runs
15 Over 104 runs 103 runs
20 Over 135 runs 144 runs
1st Inn (SL)
Session: Open PASS
10 Over 52 runs 74 runs
20 Over 117 runs 111 runs
50 Over 162 runs 171 runs
Speech Settings (Accessibility)
10% Weekly Cashback
GET iD NOW
CLICK HERE

9:55
INFO
LIVE
SCORECARD
HISTORY
Share Score
PRO TIP
You can share score screenshot by doing a long press on the live screen.
Got it, thanks
2nd Inn (SA)
Session: Open PASS
10 Over 53 runs 57 runs
15 Over 84 runs 75 runs
20 Over 97 runs 99 runs
25 Over 127 runs 132 runs
30 Over 161 runs 145 runs
35 Over 172 runs 175 runs
40 Over 206 runs 192 runs
1st Inn (AFG)
Session: Open PASS
10 Over 49 runs 41 runs
20 Over 82 runs 78 runs
30 Over 128 runs 134 runs
35 Over 160 runs 150 runs
40 Over 178 runs 173 runs
50 Over 222 runs 244 runs
Speech Settings (Accessibility)
10%
Weekly Cashback
GET iD NOW
CLICK HERE

9:55
INFO
LIVE
SCORECARD
HISTORY
Share Score
PRO TIP
You can share score screenshot by doing a long press on the live screen.
Got it, thanks
2nd Inn (AUS)
Session: Open PASS
10 Over 71 runs 58 runs
15 Over 90 runs 100 runs
20 Over 137 runs 125 runs
25 Over 161 runs 151 runs
30 Over 184 runs 179 runs
35 Over 213 runs 217 runs
40 Over 263 runs 264 runs
1st Inn (BAN)
Session: Open PASS
10 Over 48 runs 62 runs
20 Over 113 runs 114 runs
30 Over 164 runs 180 runs
35 Over 206 runs 213 runs
40 Over 243 runs 239 runs
50 Over 318 runs 306 runs
Speech Settings (Accessibility)
10% Weekly Cashback
GET iD NOW

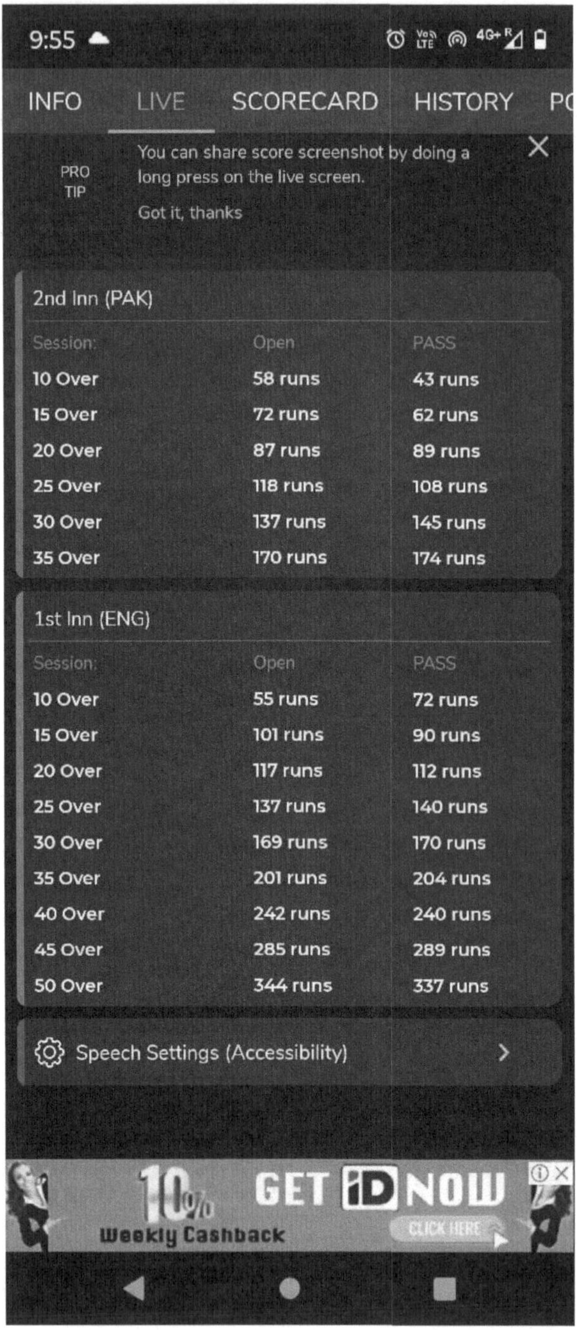

2nd Inn (PAK)

Session:	Open	PASS
10 Over	58 runs	43 runs
15 Over	72 runs	62 runs
20 Over	87 runs	89 runs
25 Over	118 runs	108 runs
30 Over	137 runs	145 runs
35 Over	170 runs	174 runs

1st Inn (ENG)

Session:	Open	PASS
10 Over	55 runs	72 runs
15 Over	101 runs	90 runs
20 Over	117 runs	112 runs
25 Over	137 runs	140 runs
30 Over	169 runs	170 runs
35 Over	201 runs	204 runs
40 Over	242 runs	240 runs
45 Over	285 runs	289 runs
50 Over	344 runs	337 runs

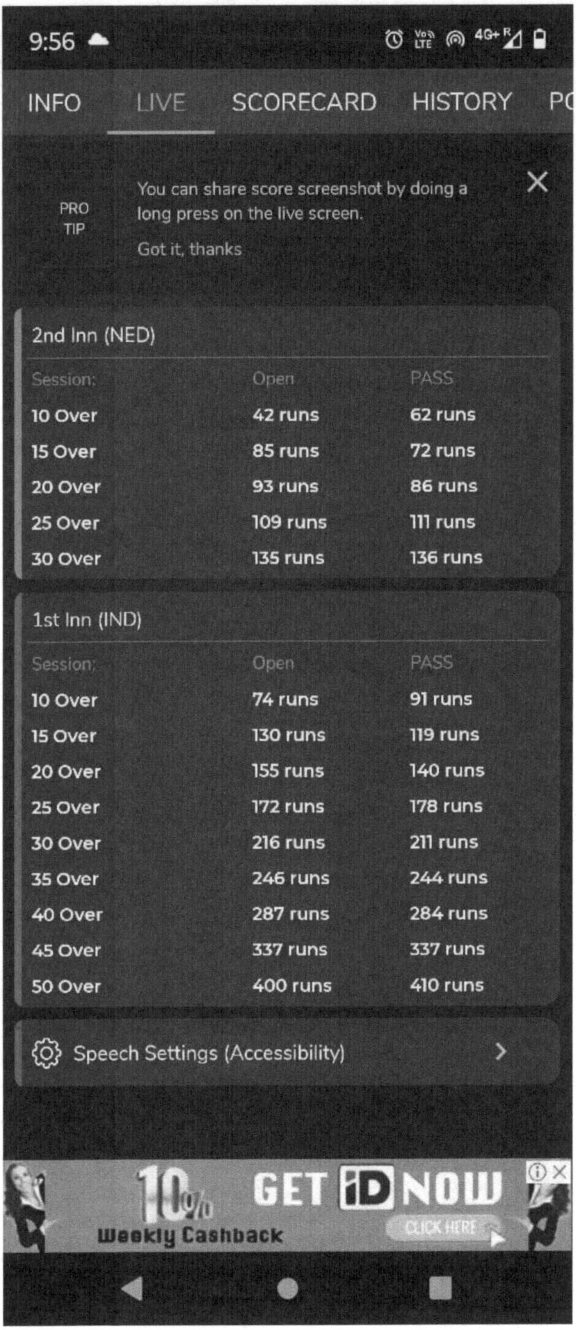
9:56
INFO
LIVE
SCORECARD
HISTORY
PRO TIP
You can share score screenshot by doing a long press on the live screen.
Got it, thanks
2nd Inn (NED)
Session: Open PASS
10 Over 42 runs 62 runs
15 Over 85 runs 72 runs
20 Over 93 runs 86 runs
25 Over 109 runs 111 runs
30 Over 135 runs 136 runs
1st Inn (IND)
Session: Open PASS
10 Over 74 runs 91 runs
15 Over 130 runs 119 runs
20 Over 155 runs 140 runs
25 Over 172 runs 178 runs
30 Over 216 runs 211 runs
35 Over 246 runs 244 runs
40 Over 287 runs 284 runs
45 Over 337 runs 337 runs
50 Over 400 runs 410 runs
Speech Settings (Accessibility)
10% Weekly Cashback
GET iD NOW
CLICK HERE

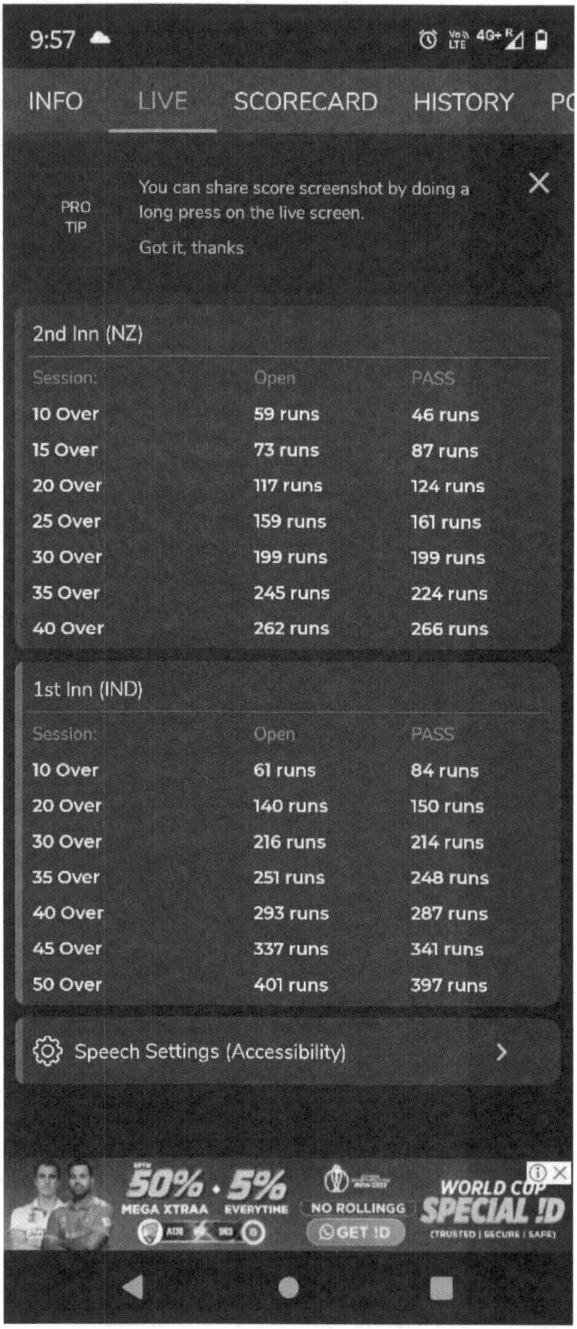
9:57
INFO
LIVE
SCORECARD
HISTORY
PRO TIP
You can share score screenshot by doing a long press on the live screen.
Got it, thanks
2nd Inn (NZ)
Session: Open PASS
10 Over 59 runs 46 runs
15 Over 73 runs 87 runs
20 Over 117 runs 124 runs
25 Over 159 runs 161 runs
30 Over 199 runs 199 runs
35 Over 245 runs 224 runs
40 Over 262 runs 266 runs
1st Inn (IND)
Session: Open PASS
10 Over 61 runs 84 runs
20 Over 140 runs 150 runs
30 Over 216 runs 214 runs
35 Over 251 runs 248 runs
40 Over 293 runs 287 runs
45 Over 337 runs 341 runs
50 Over 401 runs 397 runs
Speech Settings (Accessibility)
50% · 5%
MEGA XTRAA
EVERYTIME
NO ROLLINGG
GET ID
WORLD CUP
SPECIAL ID
(TRUSTED | SECURE | SAFE)

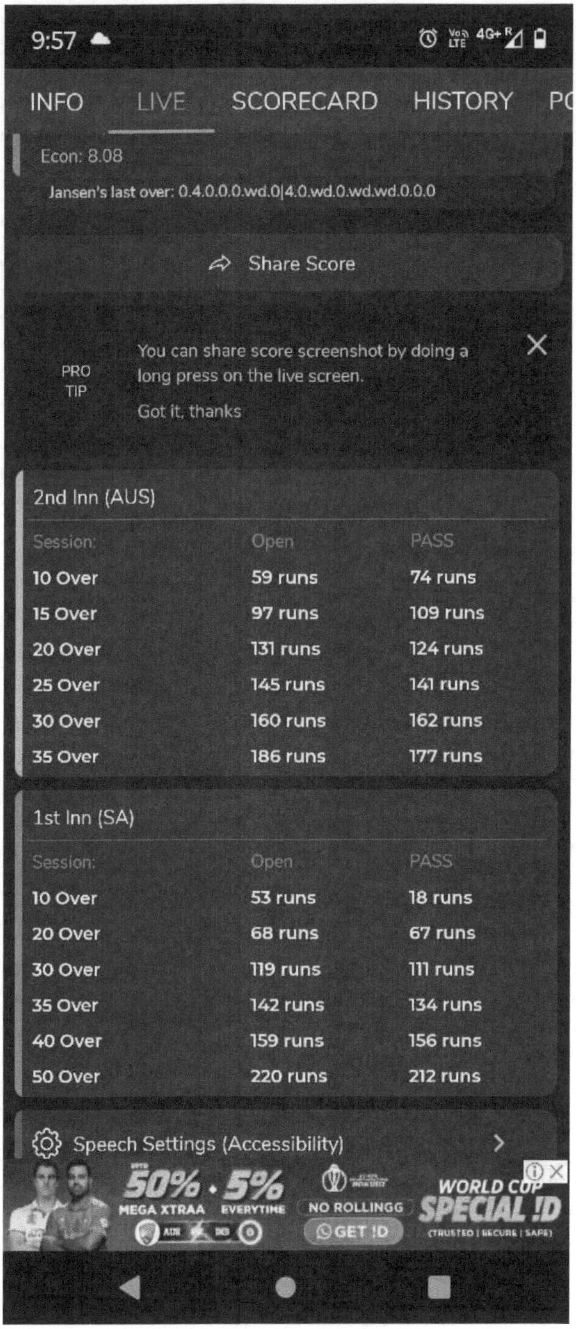
9:57
INFO
LIVE
SCORECARD
HISTORY
Econ: 8.08
Jansen's last over: 0.4.0.0.0.wd.0|4.0.wd.0.wd.wd.0.0.0
Share Score
PRO TIP
You can share score screenshot by doing a long press on the live screen.
Got it, thanks
2nd Inn (AUS)
Session: Open PASS
10 Over 59 runs 74 runs
15 Over 97 runs 109 runs
20 Over 131 runs 124 runs
25 Over 145 runs 141 runs
30 Over 160 runs 162 runs
35 Over 186 runs 177 runs
1st Inn (SA)
Session: Open PASS
10 Over 53 runs 18 runs
20 Over 68 runs 67 runs
30 Over 119 runs 111 runs
35 Over 142 runs 134 runs
40 Over 159 runs 156 runs
50 Over 220 runs 212 runs
Speech Settings (Accessibility)
50% · 5%
MEGA XTRAA EVERYTIME
NO ROLLINGG
GET ID
WORLD CUP
SPECIAL ID
(TRUSTED | SECURE | SAFE)

9:57
INFO
LIVE
SCORECARD
HISTORY
Share Score
PRO TIP
You can share score screenshot by doing a long press on the live screen.
Got it, thanks
2nd Inn (AUS)
Session: Open PASS
10 Over 55 runs 60 runs
15 Over 84 runs 78 runs
20 Over 100 runs 104 runs
25 Over 127 runs 135 runs
30 Over 165 runs 167 runs
35 Over 194 runs 192 runs
1st Inn (IND)
Session: Open PASS
10 Over 62 runs 80 runs
20 Over 133 runs 115 runs
30 Over 169 runs 152 runs
35 Over 175 runs 173 runs
40 Over 202 runs 197 runs
50 Over 274 runs 240 runs
Speech Settings (Accessibility)
50% MEGA XTRAA
5% EVERYTIME
NO ROLLINGG
GET ID
FINAL

The Final

Before the finals of the CWC 2023 played at the Narendra Modi Stadium, Ahmedabad, a narrative for India to lift the Cup had been assiduously built in India through sustained advertisements, media hype, astrologers; through social media, scores of tipsters crowding the social media; and above all through India's scripted show in the matches leading to the final. Therefore, when India lost, all the hell broke loose in India. Every Tom, Dick, and Harry was up with own reasons as to why India lost. The controversies flowed. Suddenly, the dark side of Cricket dawned on many, some suspecting that India had given away the match due to some fixing. All these jonnies would have happily or otherwise kept quiet if India had won.

So, before proceeding further or trying to know about other matches of the CWC 2023, let us see if we can know something for sure about the Final played between India and Australia. Let us straight away try to analyze some sessions of this match for the purpose.

We may see from the screenshot giving us sessions for this match in the previous chapter that when India started batting first, the session for 10 overs opened for 62 runs (that would be 61-62), and 80 runs were scored at the end of 10 overs. The number of wickets is immaterial in session betting; result is decided on the runs scored alone. But as mentioned earlier, the session being offered for betting goes on changing with the progress in a match. Thus, for these 10 overs, session score on offer for betting was 64-65 after 3.3 overs (Ind 20/0); 71 after 4 overs (Ind 30/0); 73-74 after 7.2 overs (Ind 56/1); 80-80 after 9.3 overs (Ind 76/1); 77-78 after 9.4 overs (Ind 76/2); 77 after 9.5 overs (Ind 76/2). All this is a matter of record with the various betting apps in operation. Throughout these 10 overs, the maximum score on offer was 80 and exactly 80 runs were scored at the end of these 10 overs.

As we have already seen, while betting on session, one may lay or one may back the offered score. In this case, one could lay 73 runs (i.e., one could bet against these many runs being scored at the end of the session) after 7.2 overs, or at most could lay 80 runs after 9.3 overs. Similarly, one could back 74 runs (i.e., bet for at least these many runs being scored at the end of the session) after 7.2 overs. When session on offer is with a difference of run/s between laying and backing, like 61-62 or 73-74; one loses or wins the same amount as wagered. If same score is offered for laying or backing, like 80-80 after 9.3 overs, the ratio for betting is not 1:1, it could be 110/90 (generally so) or 120/80 etc. Ratio of 110/90 would have meant that one laying the score of 80 runs would have lost Rs 1.1 and one backing it would have won Rs. 0.9 against Rs 1/- wagered.

In this session, suppose you had backed the score of 65 runs after 3.3 overs and had laid the score of 73 runs after 7.2 overs, wagering same amount each time, you would have had no risk of losing. Now suppose end score after 10 overs were 68; you would have won both your bets. Since the end score was 80, same as the maximum score that was offered throughout this session, no one could win both the bets of laying and backing, placed for whatever scores. That is because all the bets of laying would have been lost and all the bets of backing would have been won with the end score and the progress of scoring in this session as it happened.

It was a session of 60 balls and not a single bet of laying the session offer could win; since the maximum score on offer throughout the session was achieved at the end, through a 4 hit of the last ball of the session, of the 10th over.

Having come across such a scenario often many years ago, instinctively it appeared fishy and unnatural to me. I wondered what would be the probability of such a thing happening for natural/competitive cricket. Luckily or by God's grace, I could work out that probability from the basic principles of probability and natural cricket, 10 years ago. That is detailed in the book *'Bettors Beware'*, subsequently republished under the title *'All Cricket Matches are Fixed'*. One can sense that the probability of such an occurrence should be very less. I was astonished that when worked out mathematically, the probability turned out to be one in trillions. So, the scoring in the first 10 overs of the CWC final so happened or so progressed that it had probability of one in a few trillions 😮 😮 (the longer the session, the more improbable it is for such an occurrence).

Some could say, and rightly so, 'ok, that something probable once in trillion sessions happened in this one session. So what?' For their knowledge, it has earlier been seen and recorded that something like this has been happening in many sessions, so this session couldn't be that one in trillions session.

Nevertheless, let us now examine the very next session of this very match. The same screen shot tells us that this session of 20 overs opened for 133 runs and at the end only 115 runs were scored. From the records of progress in this session as available and as followed by me, the minimum score offered for laying in this session was exactly 115 which was ultimately the session score. That was ensured through only 2 runs in the 20th over and a dot ball on the last ball of the session, of the 20th over. Thus, in this session, the minimum score ever offered for laying was the ultimate session score, and one couldn't win any bet placed for backing any offered score in this session. Again, the probability of such an occurrence was same as in the first session, one in a few trillions.

So, just by looking at first two sessions of the ICC Men's CWC 2023 Final, not having to look anywhere else, one can be objectively sure, beyond any ifs and buts, that it was a thoroughly fixed and scripted match, far from a natural competitive match being played for any sort of prestige.

If this is not sufficient proof of ball-by-ball scripting or almost ball-by-ball scripting of the prestigious Final, nothing ever was proof of anything on the planet Earth.

However, the buck didn't stop after these 2 sessions. The 3rd session of 20 to 30 overs was also like the 2nd session; the minimum score ever offered for laying being the ultimate session score; 4, 3, and 3 runs were scored of the last 3 overs respectively, the last ball of the session being a dot. Similar was the fate for the session of 50 overs/innings score for India.

There were many more sessions in this match itself that defied the probability for scoring in a competitive match; but that is absolutely immaterial. Nothing else is material, since the sessions analyzed and discussed above sufficiently tell us the true nature of this match. **It is all so simple, straight, and totally objective.** The world continuing to talk all sorts of things about this match and the CWC 2023 (like https://theprint.in/opinion/stop-gloating-over-world-cup-loss-indian-team-lost-not-bjp/1854839/, https://sports.ndtv.com/icc-cricket-world-cup-2023/life-continues-kuldeep-siraj-and-rahul-react-after-world-cup-heartbreak-4599964, https://www.zee5.com/articles/when-pm-encourages-you-after-loss-it-raises-your-confidence-mohammed-shami, https://www.msn.com/en-in/sports/other/india-s-loss-in-world-cup-final-is-cricket-s-triumph-abdulrazzaq/ar-AA1kp9B7, and probably hundreds of such other) while debating about its true character or otherwise, while ignoring or unaware of the hard fact, reflects nothing but the infinite human stupidity that I have talked of in my previous writings. That should be a matter of great concern to us all!! **Some of the above referred talks are by the criminals (actors or perpetrators of the fixed match) themselves, to keep the vast populace utterly fooled.**

It should not be much difficult for anyone to understand or visualize what the above means. Even otherwise, no fixing can be in vacuum or can be vague. People just talk vaguely about a match being fixed and forget about it, without bothering to think how it was fixed or how it could be fixed. Can or would a match be scripted or fixed suddenly, after the teams having competed for some overs? **Fixing of any session necessitates ball-by-ball scripting. Otherwise, there could not be such a situation as we saw in the first three sessions of this Final.**

Now we scientifically know for sure that this Final was fixed and scripted ball-by-ball (or almost so), just as the insider Sanjeev Chawla had told the world a couple of years ago (https://www.timesnownews.com/sports/cricket/article/no-cricket-match-is-fairly-played-all-are-fixed-sanjeev-chawla-accused-bookie-hansie-cronje-fixing-scandal/599061).

Then, could such a fixing take place without the knowledge of the coaches and the administrators. Could ICC and BCCI etc. be in the dark when so precisely scripted a World Cup final was being played?

I know this will give rise to many questions in the minds of the readers. Addressing all those questions is not in the scope of this book. My previous writings serve that purpose, addressing all the possible questions, myriads of those, I hope.

After having arrived at the mathematical/scientific proof of cricket matches being fixed ball-by-ball ten years ago, and having announced it to the world through a book, and also through a press conference in the Press Club, New Delhi, India then, I never imagined that the world I lived in was so dense that the same thoroughly corrupted Cricket would still not only continue unbridled, but would continue to prosper by leaps and bounds.

While exposing it (the necessary pattern in session betting), I very well understood that the mafia controlling Cricket the world over couldn't change this and the other prevalent patterns of scoring in sessions even after being exposed, as long as session betting was in vogue. Anyone who understands session betting should be able to realize that the cricket betting industry or the betting mafia could and would go pauper if the continuous rigging of matches in a particular way (with regards to scoring patterns) didn't take place alongside the session betting.

There was no way for me to imagine then that after 10 years, I myself would be taking recourse to those efforts to tell a puzzled and dumb world that the ICC Men's CWC 2023 Final and the whole ICC Men's CWC 2023 (as we shall see in the next chapter) were nothing but stage-managed shows, no Cricket was played.

There is a marked difference between then and now, though. Then there was no record of session betting available to me; today there is no dearth of such record, it being available ball by ball.

After having conclusively known about the true character of the much hyped-up CWC 2023 Final, we may and should now reflect on some other aspects also.

Let us reflect on the odds for the match result and their movement. The opening odds of around 1.45 in favour of India against Australia didn't make much cricketing sense. I doubt if India opened with so low odds against Australia ever in a limited overs match. The basic question *'How and on what basis the betting odds are opened and continuously changed for match result?'* becomes significant and should bother us all, especially those of us who consider themselves to be the intellectuals.

As already brought out in my book *'Beat the Cricket Mafia and Win (Yes, You can do it!)'*, once a while, the mafia controlling cricket matches and cricket betting does bluff with the odds. It has to do it. Otherwise, one can almost always win by following the odds alone. This was such a match. The opening odds and their movement till the fall of the third Australian wicket indicated an Indian win (the odds were 1.3 in f/o India at that stage). That went well with all the hype built up for an Indian win, especially through the media (knowingly or unknowingly the necessary and the biggest crony of the cricket mafia). The bettors were made to feel sure about the Indian win and due to low returns available in f/o India they must have placed bets for greater amounts backing India (i.e., for an Indian win) to earn more money. The mafia made a killing in one city of India alone as per this news item in Hindi: https://www.livehindustan.com/uttar-pradesh/story-bookies-get-a-shock-of-rs-200-croresfor-those-betting-on-their-wealth-money-lost-due-to-indiadefeat-8986821.html, even though one can't be very sure about total reliability of such news.

In brief, this news story tells us that in Agra alone, the bookies earned Rs 200 crores or Rs 2 billion, the amount lost by the cricket bettors in the final. It further says that more bets flowed in favour of India after Australia lost the 3rd wicket. Also, two different news items respectively claimed that bets of Rs 50000 crores (equivalent to more than 50 billion dollars) and Rs 70000 crores (equivalent to more than 70 billion dollars) were placed in this Final. Generally, all such estimates are grossly underestimates.

It is for these astronomical sums, being wagered almost daily in various cricket matches, that the whole drama, the daily puppet shows in the name of Cricket takes/take place; other commercial gains being peanuts in comparison, being the byproducts. Yes, those commercial gains to the various participants in the mammoth fraud might be the incentive for keeping all of them glued, united in the crime.

There is another aspect also to the opening odds for this match. Prior to this match, in many matches the opening odds for India had been absurdly low and India had won one-sided, the odds further crashing fast after the start of the match. Therefore, these similar opening odds must have tempted the bettors even more to place bets for large sums backing India.

Side by side the odds for match result and sessions, the odds for various fancy bets are also taken care of. The whole ball-by-ball script is deeply/scientifically thought of and written (could be with the help of some programming/use of artificial intelligence 🤷). **Something incomprehensible to our minds conditioned otherwise; something similar to man not being able to overcome the hardened belief of sun revolving round the earth in the 16th century!**

As the 4th wicket partnership flourished in the Australian innings, the odds started jumping fast in f/o Australia (suddenly the odds became true😊) such that the bettors hardly had opportunity to cut their losses. Also, the bettors kept on expecting the next Australian wicket, which was to fall only after the match result was a foregone conclusion 😊.

The session for first 10 overs for Australian innings opened at 55 runs. Yet, after 28 runs (28/1) having been scored by Australia in the first two overs, 12 runs scored in 5 balls even after loss of the first wicket, the session on offer was just 68-69, defying any logic. On what basis did the bookies/ betting industry/mafia offer this session? What would one betting on this session instinctively do? Definitely, one would back the offered session score (only 41 runs more to be scored in next 8 overs, against the background of 28 runs scored in the first 2 overs). Feeling sure of winning at that moment by backing the session score on offer, the bettors would have lost by a margin, since the end session score was only 60. It is just one such example. It is how the betting mafia controlling the world cricket continuously fools and loots the tens of millions of bettors across the globe.

Mohammed Shami, by far the best Indian bowler so far, had the worst economy in this match. To be justified by the law of averages? A batsman of the calibre of Steven Smith is hit on the pads outside off-stump and given out LBW. And lo! He doesn't review and walks off, even though Australia had both their reviews at that moment, and it was such a crucial wicket in such a crucial match! Why on earth would Smith not review? Was this drama incorporated in the script to send a signal (grossly false) to the bettors across the world that it was India's game/ had been fixed to be India's game? For them to bet further backing India (as the above news item also mentioned)? Your guess is as good as mine😊. Most of the tipsters active on social media also were predicting Indian win since beginning of the match.😊

I watched this match also, as other matches of the World Cup, in parts only. It couldn't be possible for me to watch all the matches all the time.

Many people have come up with many reasons for India's loss in this match. Different people have blamed different players. Probably, Kohli and Rahul have borne the brunt for slow scoring. As we have seen above, they are not to blame. They were only playing the given role for the day by their masters; for the purpose of manipulation of session scores. Similarly feeding Travis Head by the bowlers on his strengths was done by the Indian bowlers as per a pre-decided script, nothing was doing of their own volition. So, all those trying to break their heads as to why India lost should now be in peace 😊.

The cricket crazy populace must understand the basics of cricket. When they frequently see highly trained bowlers bowl wayward or loose balls, or highly accomplished batters play a shot to give catch to the lone fielder in that area (when the batter could easily have scored by playing any other shot), when they see suicidal run-outs, or farcical missing of run-out chances, dolly catches being dropped etc., they should understand what was happening, without recourse to any mathematics😊. Such things may happen in natural cricket only once a while, can't be so frequent as we come across if the teams were really competing to win. The players we see are a highly trained lot, and it's not much difficult for them to get the exact result of each ball as scripted, if all in the field, including the umpires, combine and act as a bunch of actors on a movie set or in theatre.

Did it ever cross our mind, how or why it happened so frequently that a bowler bowling ordinarily suddenly bowls a ripping yorker and the batter is bowled? Or, how or why highly accomplished bowlers suddenly bowl waywardly or loose balls? Or, how or why well settled well accomplished batters suddenly play a shot to get out, mostly by giving a catching practice? Or, how or why many a batter scores a golden duck? Why suddenly matches turn such that one would be least expecting or one couldn't think of even in the wildest imagination?

While we rejoice madly on a wicket or a boundary, that particular play happens in the ground at the dictates of the betting mafia to facilitate the movement in the various betting odds as suited it.

❒

The ICC Men's CWC 2023

On the very outset, just try to find out how many runs were scored, or how many boundaries were hit of numerous free-hit balls in the ICC Men's CWC 2023, you should get all your answers about genuineness of this highly publicized World Cup, if you apply common-sense or cricketing sense😊 😊. If you also try to see the recordings of shots played on these balls, you should understand even better.

One should also contemplate as to suddenly how and why the world beater English Cricket team forgot Cricket and forgot how to bat, to lose match after match in their initial encounters, something the least expected of them. Same England later on defeated a strong Pakistan in a thoroughly one-sided contest from beginning till end, in a must-win match for Pakistan.😊

After pursuing the last chapter, many could say, without thinking much, "May be just the Final of the CWC 2023 was fixed; that doesn't mean that the whole WC was fixed." On the face of it, their contention may appear to be well placed, but let us try to apply some common-sense. We have already seen through application of our mind that such a prestigious Final couldn't be fixed without the blessings of ICC and other authorities. If that were not so, we would have seen ICC and the other authorities in action by now against the mega-fraud. If ICC and the authorities had been meaning well, they would have acted 10 years ago on my public exposures and on my various mails to ACU (Anti-Corruption Unit) of ICC and subsequently to a number of other authorities.

It is a matter of record through my books and other writings in the public domain as to how all the matches of Cricket in various prestigious leagues and also the international matches were always scripted. So, not the naive, but only dumb-witted would think that other matches of the World Cup were fair and square, while the Final was fixed and scripted.

Let us forget all that and examine the other matches of the CWC 2023 on their own merit also. The opening odds and sessions for these matches have been brought out in a previous chapter. The readers may analyze various sessions in these matches on their own, from the score books available, to see objectively for themselves whether natural cricket was played or not. However, I shall mention some more pertinent things that came to my notice, that occurred to me, during the course of following these World Cup matches off and on.

In many matches of the CWC 2023, the opening odds didn't make much logical sense, as we can see from the odds for all the matches given in an earlier chapter, but proved to be alright as the match progressed. In most of the matches, the teams that were much favourite as per the opening odds went on to win very comfortably, the opposite team hardly ever appearing to be in competition, or appeared to be in competition only for a short while, especially as per the movement of the odds😊. For example, in the group match between India and New Zealand, both the teams had been playing well and were unbeaten in the tournament before their clash. And in previous World Cup matches between the two teams, New Zealand had won more times, also having won last such encounter between the two teams. And yet, the odds opened much in favour of India, at around 1.5. The match progressed as per these odds.😊

The matches number 2 to 9, 11, 12, 14, 16 to 19, 21, 23, 24, 27, 31 to 34, 36, 37, 40 to 42, 44, 45, and the two semi finals were such matches, i.e., 32 out of total 48 matches, where the teams with the opening odds much in their favour won very comfortably, in one-sided or almost one-sided contests. In some of these matches like match number 37 between Australia and New Zealand, though it might have appeared keen/even contest to the viewers at times, yet the odds remained one-sided throughout. The bookies/ those controlling the odds knew beforehand for all these matches as to how these were to progress. Many would retort instantly, “But for remaining 16 matches they didn’t know.” They would be grossly wrong. Those controlling the odds knew and know for each and every match. They can’t allow the teams opening with favourite odds to win each and every time. If so, the bettors would always back such teams and will win all their bets. The bettors have to be kept guessing all the time.

Probably, match number 39, between Australia and Afghanistan, was the most specially scripted match of this World Cup, both for the bettors and the other viewers. 😊 The odds after toss were 1.18 in f/o Australia who ultimately won the match. For the viewers, Australia snatched win from the jaws of defeat, after they were 91/7 while chasing 292 to win. Mitchell Starc, inexplicably, walked off as the 7th wicket without reviewing after being given out caught behind. Could he not know that he had not hit the ball? Odds after his wicket were around 1.01 in f/o Afghanistan. Australia won from thereon without losing any further wicket, with Maxwell allowed to hit sixes at will by the dreaded Afghanistan spinners and other bowlers. Something like Starc walking off was to repeat in the Final when Smith walked off (mentioned in the previous chapter). Similar thing happened in the Semifinal between SA and Australia, when in the 44th over of the South African innings, Coetzee didn't review on being given out caught behind, even though the ball had brushed his upper arm; SA lost the match this time.

To add to the drama, and probably to make it an excuse later on for Afghanistan to lose from such a situation, and probably also to make the bettors more assured that next wicket would fall any time; two catches of Maxwell were dropped in quick succession, not much after the 7th wicket, one of those being a dolly dropped by Mujeeb.

Seemingly Afghanistan again lost opportunity for a semifinal berth when the same appeared to be for the taking, somewhat like the last Asia Cup. Both times, the loss by Afghanistan was self-inflicted at the end. **But all that is only for our consumption. Afghanistan reaching such strong positions also was result of a script, as was their dramatic suicidal losses in the end.**

In the 43rd match between Bangladesh and Australia also, the initial favourite Australia won comfortably in the end, even though Bangladesh appeared to be well in contention having posted 306 runs batting first, the odds even then were inexplicably around only 1.4 in f/o Australia. As the bookies already knew, Australia chased down this 300 plus score quite easily. Most of the bettors, expecting some competition at some stage at least, must have counted their losses in this World Cup match also. In the 29th match between India and England also, the starting favourites India won quite comfortably in the end, though at one stage England were much favourites before losing first wicket while chasing.

Thus, the teams expected by the bookies to win before start of a match won most of the times. The readers may now like to go back to the preface and the initial chapters literally or in their mind.

The mafia doesn't only control the opening odds, but also their movement with the progress of the matches. Many a time, the movement of betting odds clearly gives away the fact of Cricket being in the grip of the betting mafia to anyone who is watchful enough and has an open mind.

In the match between Afghanistan and India played on the 11th October, 2023, Afghanistan were batting first. With their fourth wicket partnership in full flow, the odds for India had jumped up to 1.4 after the 32nd over (Afghanistan 161/3). In the 33rd over, further 12 runs were scored with a 6 being hit of the last ball of the over, and yet the odds for India or in f/o India had come down to 1.31. That was absurd on the face of it (the odds for India must have increased to be much above 1.4), but the bookies/mafia knew better. The partnership got broken soon after in the 35th over and despite Afghanistan posting a healthy 272/8 in the allotted 50 overs, India went on to win too comfortably (as the opening odds and the movement of odds throughout this match had meant).

Similarly, when batting first against India, Bangladesh were a very promising 93/0 in the 15th over, the odds were only 1.33 in f/o India (meaning that as per the bookies, even then probability of India winning was 300 % or 3 to 1). How did the betting mafia know beforehand that it was going to be a cake walk for India from there on? How does the mafia or the betting industry know so well, even though Cricket is said to be a game of glorious uncertainties? In the Semifinal between India and New Zealand, even when New Zealand appeared to be on course in chasing down the mammoth Indian total, with 219/2 after the 32nd over, and many Indian viewers were feeling jittery, the betting mafia knew very well what was to come. One, even then the odds in f/o India were below 1.2. Two, the odds suddenly came down to 1.14 a bit before fall of the 3rd wicket (that had nothing to do with pitch siding or time lag between actual play and the telecast).

In the group match between India and New Zealand, India were chasing 274 to win. In the 35th over of Indian innings, when the TV screens were showing win prediction for India at 60%, the bookies knew much better. Odds in f/o India then were only 1.44 (as per win prediction, these should have been around 1.67), and India went on to win comfortably from there on.

There are odds for the match result and the innings score for the first innings on offer for every match. As mentioned earlier, both of these go on changing as a match progresses. There should be a continuous logical correlation between the two, especially in a limited overs match. But, in many matches, that correlation disappears midway, and it also happened so in this World Cup. Even though the ultimate first innings score was less than what was expected at the start for the favourite team batting first on many occasions, the odds for it went even further down substantially (by way of percentage); and the opposite team didn't even remotely compete. A few examples are the matches between New Zealand and Netherlands, New Zealand and Afghanistan, India and Netherlands, England and Netherlands etc. Such a thing happens very often to continuously fool the bettors round the globe. Those balancing their bets between the match result and the session scores get deceived again and again.

Scoring throughout the World Cup had to proceed as per the dictates of Session manipulation and it did so. With most of the betting websites supporting 5 overs sessions, at least in the first innings, betting took place on hundreds of sessions in the World Cup. Therefore, one could easily see the session manipulation galore.

Let us look at a few examples. 13 runs were scored of the last ball in the New Zealand innings vs Netherlands for manipulation of the innings score. Almost all the no-balls for height, wide balls, front foot no-balls etc. are bowled on purpose, sometimes too obvious, for session manipulations (you will often find such things happening in the last over of a session, or towards the very end of a session) or for other purposes. One can often see bowlers casually bowling wide balls to lose a match after the chasing had become somewhat tight.

Sudden batting collapses, or tailenders hitting at will or late partnerships after the top batters having flopped, often happen for session (innings score) manipulations along with manipulation of the match result and of other fancy bets. Some such examples in this World Cup were: sudden collapse of Pakistan against India, of Afghanistan against Bangladesh, of Bangladesh scoring well after the match was virtually over against South Africa, in contrast Netherlands folding up cheaply against Australia the very next day; collapses of Sri Lanka, England, and SA against India beyond imagination (these might also have served the purpose of bettors expecting similar collapse of Australia in the final 😊); Sri Lanka managing only 344 runs/9 wickets against Pakistan after being 229/3 after 30 overs etc.

Chasing 358 to win against India, Sri Lanka scored 14/6 in first 10 overs (10th over being a double wicket maiden), the minimum offered session score throughout the session (also a session beyond one's wildest imagination); chasing exactly same score to win against SA the previous day, New Zealand scored 67/3 in 15 overs, the minimum offered session score throughout the session for that session; in the same match, SA well achieved the highest offered session score for 50 overs through a 6 of the last ball; a day before Bangladesh was all out for 204 against Pakistan, to score the minimum innings score offered by the bookies. These are some other examples.

Many times, it happens that if session score of x-(x+1) is offered at the end of last or second last over preceding the session or in the beginning, exactly x runs are scored so that the bookies win all the bets placed at that point of time. Suppose a 20 over session score given by the bookies is 95-96 at the end of the 18th or the 19th over. These are the moments that many bets are placed for the session. Since a bettor can either bet against 95 runs being scored (that is for less than 95 runs being scored) or for 96 or more runs being scored, the bookie wins all the bets placed that time if the end session score is exactly 95. One could come across many such instances also in this long World Cup. Just as an example, after 2 overs, 5 overs session for Afghanistan against India was 19-20. Afghanistan had scored 18 runs after 4 overs; only 1 run was scored of the 5th over for session score to be exactly 19. For another example, 30 overs session for England against India at the end of the 29th over was 101-102; the score at the end of 30 overs was exactly 101 (101/8).

Most of the times, scoring in the end overs of a session takes place against the run of play till then; to fool the millions and millions of innocent and ignorant punters who go on betting taken in by the run of play, expecting normal competitive Cricket, and expecting that the teams were playing to win etc.

Self-defeating decisions by the captains on winning the toss, like Sri Lanka deciding to bat first against Australia on the 16th October 2023, even though 80% of the times team bowling first had won there (Sri Lanka scored much below par and went on to lose in a one-sided contest), Netherlands choosing to bat against Sri Lanka (pitch was supposed to help the fast bowlers early on) etc.; players particularly chosen for the day to perform a conspicuous role, mostly of under-performance leading to the team's defeat, like Usama Mir playing for Pakistan against Australia, Baresi replacing Vikram Singh for Netherlands in the match against Afghanistan etc.; inexplicable reviews by teams, like by Australia on the first ball against Sri Lanka, or New Zealand reviewing for LBW in the very first over against Afghanistan even when the ball pitched way outside leg, Pakistan reviewing for LBW against Australia of the first ball etc.; inexplicably not taking of the reviews (some examples already given above) by the teams like Australia not taking a review in the 10th over against Sri Lanka for Perera to be LBW etc.; and inexplicable running between the wickets etc. were all amply on show in this World Cup.

The discerning viewers could very frequently see in this World Cup how the bowlers bowled loose balls on purpose; like Dutt of Netherlands bowling four consecutive short and wide balls to be hit for four consecutive fours by David Warner, Mohammad Nawaz of Pakistan bowling a rank loose ball to lose an all-important match against SA etc.

Throughout the various matches, it was also not much difficult to see the batsmen playing shots on purpose to get out. The same was amply visible in almost every match. Many times, it was too obvious to any critical viewer. For example, the shots played by Ackerman and Edwards in the Netherlands' match against New Zealand; the shots played by Bairstow and Root in England's capitulation to South Africa, etc.

The suicidal run-outs were also sufficiently on show in the CWC 2023. The Netherlands batsmen probably had the maximum share of that, match after match. Similarly, on show was the farcical missing of run-out chances. Probably Phehlukwayo of SA missing run-out in the 23rd over against Afghanistan, and Mohammad Nabi of Afghanistan breaking stumps in the 30th over against Sri Lanka with hands to avoid run-out will get the cake.

The experts through pitch report etc. and the captains through their utterances at the toss quite frequently mislead the viewers and deceive the bettors among them. In the New Zealand vs Australia match, the experts were telling of swing initially; and yet batting first, Australia scored 118 runs in the first 10 overs. In the match between Netherlands and Bangladesh, we were told by Rameej Raja before start that the pitch was a solid batting pitch and a high scoring contest/match was on the cards. Batting first, Netherlands scored only 229 runs and while chasing, Bangladesh got bundled out for 142 runs. In Bangladesh vs Pakistan match, giving the pitch report, Shane Watson told us that pitch was going to crack and offer turn, and it was going to be a challenge for the batters. And yet, Pakistan chased town the target of 205 runs with consummate ease.

In Australia vs Bangladesh match, after winning the toss and choosing to bowl, the Australian captain Pat Cummins expected early help for the bowlers. Just the opposite happened, and Bangladesh scored well in the first 10 overs without losing any wicket. One could have come across many such instances in this World Cup. Such reports or utterances can't always be wrong for the obvious reasons. 😊

I repeat, the above mentions by me are not exhaustive, these are barely indicative, to give the readers a sufficient idea of the fakeness of the subject World Cup, and of all that happens so that they can be wiser as a bettor or otherwise. Also, all the aspects, like purposeful deceit by the commentators etc., might have not been covered. The examples of all the aspects are there in abundance in my earlier writings, the same were again on show aplenty in this long World Cup, spanning 48 matches of 50 overs a side. **The subject of cricket betting and correspondingly all the necessary fixing is as vast and deep as an ocean.**

In short, the betting odds/session betting etc. are not governed by plays in the field as would appear to anyone; but the plays in the field are pre-scripted to suit how the betting mafia had decided the odds and session scores etc. to move or behave. Side by side, the façade of Cricket has to continue. **It continues with the aid of the cricketers and ex-cricketers, superb acting by the players, pretence of on-field fighting and sledging among them, with the aid of the commentators, the cricket experts and administrators etc. It is also well aided by the ignorant, dense, or hand-in-glove authorities; by the ignorant, dumb or unconcerned masses, the corporate world, the celebrities, and the political leaders etc.** The purpose of amassing billions of dollars for the betting mafia daily gets easily served.

Most of the viewers, instinctively or as a result of their continuous conditioning since childhood, discard the possibility of institutional ball-by-ball (it's almost ball-by-ball) scripting of Cricket matches, without applying mind and with no efforts for trying to know and grasp the truth. They just watch some matches casually and live with the impressions formed in their minds from what they see. Also, there are many things they come across which are beyond their comprehension as to how those could be scripted. **Yes, but irrespective of all that, we scientifically know for sure that there has to be institutional, almost ball-by-ball, fixing of the cricket matches on show that are available for betting and session betting.** So, there has to be some explanation for everything else, that must be well-known to the perpetrators of the continuous fake Cricket.

Two, let people apply mind and think - if it is not complete institutional fixing, precisely how does partial fixing take place in the open matches, remaining unknown to so many cricket experts and the authorities😊 😊? Let them try to come out with clear answers. How can it be possible for the same players/teams to play fixed cricket sometimes, and compete at other times in the same match? Why do the viewers come across so many instances of farcical or inexplicable occurrences in the field, with no one there to ask any questions? Many intelligent minds should get to understand the reality.

The readers should also know of Steven Smith of Australia being given out LBW against SA by the on-field umpire and the decision being confirmed also through Hawkeye when reviewed. His total bewilderment on such a decision is well known. There was some talk about it in social media also (bit.ly/46M7UTI). A heading 'Aussies Fume as DRS changes Law of Physics' did the rounds in the aftermath of this.

The implications of totally corrupt Cricket going on unbridled all around us are too vast and grave. And yet, when someone, who bothers about many other petty wrongdoings around him/her, says, "What is it to me? Why should I bother?" or things like that; that someone touches the heights of stupidity or imbecility. We shall see more of it in the next chapters.

Abusing the National Anthems

The practice of both the competing teams singing/reciting their national anthems was followed in each and every match of the World Cup 2023. Since every match was scripted, one of the two teams losing on purpose, as we have seen conclusively; didn't that singing amount to openly abusing their national anthem by the participating teams? Every team lost one or another match in this World Cup knowingly or on purpose, thus abusing their national anthem at least once.

While the national anthems of the participating 10 countries were openly abused in the Men's CWC 2023, **side by side all their countrymen stood grossly cheated, including around one and a half billion Indians.** In fact, same would apply to the qualifying matches also. Could it be Cricket that the West Indies, seemingly having so many world beaters in their ranks, didn't even qualify for this World Cup?😊

Some of the masses, cheated thus even committed suicide, a few of them being reported also: https://www.indiatvnews.com/west-bengal/news-world-cup-final-india-australia-two-die-by-suicide-after-india-loss-to-australia-west-bengal-odisha-latest-updates-2023-11-21-903655. One can safely assume that most of such suicides, especially of the heavily losing bettors across the globe, won't have found way in the media news.

It didn't matter whether a team belonged to a first world or a third world country. **In cheating their respective populace,**

all the teams and the countries were one. The cheating and fraud united them all as nothing else, beyond religion, class, or nationality.

The above is a clear and a very big accusation, there is nothing half-hearted about it. I take this opportunity to challenge the whole world to haul me over the coals, if I am wrong.😊

❐

A Cop in Cricket

This is the title of a book by Mr. Neeraj Kumar, IPS, who retired as police commissioner of Delhi. He is much known in the cricketing world for having handled the infamous Sreesanth spot-fixing case of IPL 6 in the year 2013. After his retirement, he was offered to head the ACU (Anti-Corruption Unit) of BCCI (Board of Control for Cricket in India), and consequently he worked in that capacity for 3 years from June 2015 to May 2018. The above book, published in 2023, has been written by him to tell us about the inside world of the BCCI's anti-corruption unit. Unfortunately, the book gives far from a rosy picture about the BCCI, its anti-corruption unit, and the erstwhile Head of the COA for BCCI, Mr. Vinod Rai.

It was by chance that I came to know of the existence of this book recently, in the midst of drafting the present book. I got a copy and read it word by word. The book was an eye-opener for me about Mr. Neeraj Kumar. From the handling of the Sreesanth case (as detailed in the chapter 'Large Scale Fixing Gets Established but All look the Other Way' in my book 'Bettors Beware' of 2013, subsequently republished under the title 'All Cricket Matches are Fixed'), and the fact of institutionally fixed Cricket having continued as such during his tenure as ACU chief and afterwards, I didn't have a good opinion about him as far as Cricket was concerned. But this book very clearly tells what a man he has been! He has done his utmost to fight all around corruption in Cricket against all the odds. One can easily sense his unimpeachable integrity and extra-ordinary intentions and efforts through the pages of this book. Now I also know what an illustrious career he has had as an IPS (Indian Police Service) officer!

When someone like Mr. Neeraj Kumar writes a book, it is with utmost sense of responsibility. This book should leave no doubt in any mind about the sad character of BCCI, the all-powerful body that controls Cricket-more than a religion- in India. **What saddens me probably even more is the revelation from this book that even persons like Mr. Neeraj Kumar, a top IPS officer with great achievements, having overseen the investigations in the Sreesanth case, and so closely connected with Cricket and the top cricketers for years, could not even remotely have an idea about the reality of international cricket and the cricketers.** Even worse, he had in all probability no knowledge of the continuous exposes on the subject over last 10 years, of the PIL in the Supreme Court of India (even though he was in BCCI at that time) etc. To my mind, he has simply been ignorant. And just think of tens of millions of other intellectuals, thousands of them being great achievers in their chosen fields! They, otherwise the leaders in the society, continue to be fooled day and night by the rogues of the cricket world, due to their ignorance. **And they don't feel any qualms about having been so utterly fooled 24 × 7 all their life, even when they become aware later on.**

Through his book, Mr. Neeraj Kumar tells us about private leagues like Rajwada Cricket League and Rajputana Premier League. He narrates how even untrained eyes could see the rampant corruption through scripted plays in these leagues, organized and played only for the benefit of the bookies/ betting websites. He mentions that full-toss balls, no balls, absurd field settings, dropped catches and far too mix-ups in running between the wickets were frequent. He mentions how 17 runs and 11 runs were conceded in the last over to facilitate the win by the chasing teams.

Interestingly, what Mr. Neeraj Kumar told us about these private leagues, happens as a routine not only in other prestigious leagues wherein reputed international cricketers of the present or past participate, but all such things and many more, like batters playing shots to get out, bowlers bowling balls for getting hit for boundaries or over boundaries, farcical missing of run-outs, the batsmen not appealing for review on being given out when they must have known that the umpire's decision was wrong, dubious umpiring and flimsy Hawkeyes etc. were amply on show in the most prestigious Men's CWC 2023 (some examples given in the last chapter) also.

At times, all the above being on purpose was too obvious. And that was being done by the top international players. All these things are amply on show in the ongoing Legends League (November, 2023) as I write this, in which star cricketers or legends of the game like Gayle, Gautam Gambhir, Pathan brothers etc. are participating.

Probably the viewers fail to note all these things because they are never viewing a match critically or with their own eyes. **They see matches only for fun, they see through the eyes of the commentators or what the commentators want them to see and make them see.** Moreover, remaining ignorant, they just can't and don't imagine that such things could be happening at that level, **that all the cricket they were so crazy about could being played primarily for the benefit of an unknown betting mafia, just like the private leagues mentioned by Mr. Neeraj Kumar.**

Mr. Neeraj Kumar has mentioned about 17 and 11 runs being given away/ scored in the last over as something obviously fishy, he must have meant the way these runs were allowed. One comes across such things and much worse in top and prestigious leagues and international matches very often. In a match in IPL-2023 only, 5 consecutive sixes were allowed to be hit in the last 5 balls, to lose the match by a team.😄 The opposite also happens quite often. The teams fail to score the required winning runs, that appeared to be a cake walk, for no rhyme or reason. Examples abound.

It doesn't matter at all to those controlling Cricket as to how farcical or unbelievable script is presented at what level. Because they know very well that there is no one to ask any questions. The people, especially in India, continue to be crazy about Cricket, continuously fooled by Shastris and Gavaskars, and the bettors across the globe continue to lose heavily to the betting mafia. The mafia is assured of the full support of the authorities, especially those controlling Cricket, and of the media to be on its side, **or of them being thorough imbeciles like most of the cricket journalists.**

The viewers also fail to apply mind that if so many balls were palpably fishy, that couldn't be in isolation and had to be a part of some overall script. Of course, we have already seen conclusively how the whole ICC Men's CWC 2023 was out and out scripted, as the cricket has been for last some decades.

There is something puzzling. A Police Officer, an IPS, of the calibre of Mr. Neeraj Kumar has mentioned in his book that the cricket betting was illegal in India. He has also opined against making it legal. But the judgement in the Sreesanth case which he himself has quoted in his book, had also said this:

"267 The game of cricket, therefore, cannot be held as a game of chance, but is a game of skill which is exempted under Section 12 of Public Gambling Act, from the definition of Gambling.

268 Therefore, even if it is accepted that there was rampant betting going on in the IPL6, but it is an activity excluded u/s 12 of Public Gambling Act, and is not an offence for which any of the accused can be held liable."

I have deliberated in some detail on this judgement in my book *'Beat the Cricket Mafia and Win (Yes, You can do it!)'*.

Apart from the above paras 267 and 268 in the mentioned judgement, scores of cricket betting sites are openly functioning in India for years. The hundreds of tipsters are openly active on the social media. It can't be that the law-enforcers of India know nothing about all this. Not only that, the cricket betting is also being advertised in a big way. The following full page (first page) ad appeared in a leading Hindi daily of India on the 21st January, 2023 (or there abouts).

This one website alone, out of scores of such large and small (by way of business) websites was announcing one crore or 10 million plus users.

The cricket betting remaining in grey area in India, in all probability being deliberately done so, the tens/hundreds of millions of addicted bettors remain at the mercy of the betting sites and hence the betting mafia. They are taken for a ride quite often, in more ways than one. People have even shared their experiences of having been fleeced by popular betting sites on the social media. **That alone, to my mind, is a big reason enough to legalise betting in India without further loss of time.** The culpability of the present government in this regard has already been brought out in my earlier writings.

In this regard, a recent interview of said to be cricket betting magnate Amit Majithia with one Mr Wahiid Ali Khan (https://youtu.be/qySBjaLqVhk?si=6eX5Xt9zUNLkFnw9), reciprocates the above, though its contents with regards to cricket fixing are grossly misleading for the masses as usual and are devoid of much sense.

I succeeded in contacting Mr Neeraj Kumar after having come to know of his latest book. And did make him aware of my books, especially the latest one, and the website **thecricketmafia.com.** The purpose was to try to make at least people like him aware of what was what. **A person like him becoming interested in the crusade against the colossal open fraud could be a big way forward.** He did respond sportingly initially, but stopped responding later on, by the time I completed his book, for the reasons best known to him. My query to him regarding the legality of betting also remained unanswered. Everyone has own reasons, limitations, and compulsions!

❑

The Dense World

If the world we live in were not so dense as it is, there won't have been any need for this book. In fact, there won't have been any need for my previous books or for books by other authors on the subject of the darker side of Cricket, after the book *'Bettors Beware'* was published in 2013. **Is it not one of the greatest wonders that the same thoroughly scripted and fixed Cricket is continuing today with aplomb and with ever increasing pomp and show, even after having been publicly exposed and having been so proven scientifically ten years ago?**

In the previous chapter, I have mentioned about the continuing ignorance on the subject, of the hundreds of millions of otherwise well-meaning men and women. Worse than these ignorant men and women, with no fault of theirs, are the blind and the imbeciles. They also abound. I may be detested for saying so, but most of those in contact with me over the years through social media or otherwise will fall in this category. Who have chosen to remain blind till they die are those who would rather go by their misplaced belief than opening their eyes and applying mind to what was being said, why, and with what authority.

They would rather not bother that someone among them had proved everything even scientifically. They are quite aware that someone was telling the reality of cricket for years. **But their ego doesn't let them listen to an ordinary mortal; they have been tutored all their life to listen to the media and the**

authorities alone, howsoever rogue they may be. They remain ignorant out of their choice. They tell themselves, "Why should I bother whether Cricket is fixed or not? I enjoy the drama." Apparently, they have no self-respect. Leaving alone the deep and vast implications that do affect them in many ways, being so grossly fooled publicly for decades doesn't matter to them. Most of the world is like that.

Then there are imbeciles who try but fail to grasp the reality, because it is against their hardened belief. Something quite like what happened in the 16th century when for about 100 years man couldn't grasp and accept the scientific fact of the earth revolving round the sun. The fact of cricket being all scripted and being like a puppet show also lies scientifically and even otherwise proved in the public domain for last 10 years. Yet, the ignorant, the blind, and the imbeciles don't know, don't want to understand, or don't understand what is what. Probably they should not be blamed, because the reality is so extra-ordinary, and the public is continuously bombarded day and night through the media with the opposite, with the falsity, that it becomes very difficult for them to comprehend the highly explosive truth. The people tend even to ignore the scientifically proven facts, **giving precedence to what they believe or what they are made to believe by the vested interests.**

Despite some glaring similarity, there is a very big material difference between what happened in the 16th century and what has been happening now for last 10 years in the 21st century. Then it was about not accepting a very significant astronomical fact related to our own planet. The life on the planet continued as usual with that haughty ignorance as it had been continuing before. But in the 21st century, due to similar or even worse human stupidity, a proven daily fraud worth tens of billions of dollars has been continuing unbridled. **It has been adversely affecting**

the lives of tens or hundreds of millions of bettors directly in many ways besides the substantial monetary losses, and has been influencing the rest of the world indirectly but quite badly, resulting in the loss of many a life also as we have seen. I go nuts when I think of the apathy of all sorts of authorities and of millions and millions of intellectuals endowed with an acute brain toward this mammoth known and proven public fraud, prospering every day. Waking up to the reality 10 years back, as it must have happened, would have saved the human world a lot of miseries, and would have turned it topsy-turvy for a much better further evolution since then!!

To my mind, the worst lot is of those, almost all the intellectuals or not so intellectuals I have come across would fall in this category, who feel and say that it's not something they should bother about at all. It is alright for them to bother about all other petty (comparatively not even pea-nuts) wrong-doings that are brought to their notice through the media, but they must not bother about the tens of billions of dollars a day open public fraud, facilitated by the media itself. They will break their head on historical events, on every other happening around them, and will show off their wisdom every now and then, at the least given opportunity. They are the worst type of imbeciles the human world is full of. Last 10 long years have amply established their existence. I am sure, any such realisation only would have led Einstein to comment out of exasperation, *"Two things are infinite: the universe and human stupidity; and I'm not sure about the universe."*

I liked the video 'https://www.youtube.com/live/8xh5Hzm-1Rr4?si=LgQePKQ2t0KjqfWx' for what Mr. RVS Mani says towards the end. He said that being quite aware that the cricket matches (should be continuous) matches were like a drama or movies, he didn't watch Cricket, but was quite concerned about it being what it was, it meant and it led to. Mr. Sree Iyer also rightly said that betting was the root cause for Cricket to be what it is, exactly what was said by me in the book '*Bettors Beware*' 10 years ago. The video also showed that though rightly suspecting present day Cricket to be thoroughly corrupt, both of these gentlemen were highly ignorant of the whole reality. They knew nothing about session betting and not much about betting, yet they were aware of and told some truth, not knowing the whole truth by far. Persons like them also not knowing what was what still, also exhibited the denseness of the human world.

The social media was abuzz a lot in the aftermath of India losing the final, since India's win was being taken for granted by vast majority of the cricket fans in India, as mentioned earlier. Therefore, the shocking defeat of India resulted in all sorts of people to mushroom, especially in India, for analysing the reasons for India's loss. **These scores of analyses and analysts further showed how dense the human world was.** No one knew what had happened why, the forces behind it, despite it all having been in the public domain for years and years, and yet everyone considered himself/herself to be an expert. Probably this video sums it up very well: https://youtu.be/bFIj-94IYn8?feature=shared. The anchor is too ignorant, knows nothing, is talking a lot of balderdash with great confidence, attempting cheap politicisation.

The readers may also sample this post being forwarded on whatsapp/social media after India's loss in the Final:

"The World notices the exclusive narrow mindedness of Modi's India.

The Sydney Morning Herald and The Guardian London comments on How India has taken the World out of the ICC Cricket World Cup.

Its a World Cup for India, by India and for Indians. It is also the most small- hearted and petty one ever hosted.

Unlike any other world cup, there were no fans from foreign countries. No other flags except the Indian flag being waved. All matches not featuring India had empty stands and no spectators.

120,000 fans at the Narendra Modi stadium sang the national anthem and chanted Jai Sri Ram Perhaps the listless performance of other teams reflects their dislike of the game being used as a tool to frame political messages with all the subtlety of a sledgehammer.

Monal Desai

It is not only the World Cup we lost last night.

We lost the respect of the World for pettiness, unmatched in any World Cup seen so far

Endless brickbats for @BCCI under @JayShah as the #GracelessGujus and their Judwa mentors show their embarrassing colours at the #ICCCricketWorldCup2023Final

A "pathetic" act at the end of the Cricket World Cup has sparked outrage with the world turning on those responsible.

The most shocking act came when on-field umpires Richard Kettleborough and Richard Illingworth were called to the podium to receive their mementos — only to be booed by the remaining crowd for no apparent reason.

The commentator behind the high profile Edgar Allan Poe's Twitter account posted: "I could not believe my ears but they BOOED THE UMPIRES????"

It was one of several acts from the crowd that have caused outrage, including the moment Aussie hero Travis Head brought up his hundred .. the local crowd gave him nothing when he raised his bat.

"The empty seats once India starts losing, the inability to cheer for a spectacular innings and a well deserved World Cup win, booing the umpires, shouting Kohli Kohli when their players are being announced, and now this. This has been so deeply embarrassing. And on the world stage."

Ricky Ponting on Sky Sports:

"Even with so much control and hold over world cricket, India has lost yet another tournament. Money can't buy success & time and time again teams like Australia, New Zealand and Pakistan have proved that." "

What absolute imbecility!! Such things are talked about, and engage the intellectuals; no one bothering about the real relevant thing that the Cricket World Cup, so much show-cased throughout the world for over a month, was totally fake. **Or are such reactions as above deliberately triggered at the behest of the mafia to keep the reality camouflaged and the world fooled, kept engaged in non-issues and non-sense?** Comments by people like Ponting, someone having to be in full knowledge of the fake Cricket and hence the fake World Cup would indicate so.

All above is similar to ball tampering and other controversies in Cricket hogging the headlines for months; but nowhere a word being mentioned about the real basic thing, about Cricket itself being totally fake. Post CWC 2023, the newspapers and TV channels were full of all sorts of talks like https://timesofindia.indiatimes.com/sports/cricket/icc-world-cup/news/sudhar-jao-yaar-mohammed-shami-slams-ex-pakistan-players-for-creating-controversies-during-world-cup/

articleshow/105408675.cms, https://www.indiatvnews.com/sports/cricket/danish-kaneria-former-pakistan-cricketer-lauds-pm-modi-for-consoling-team-india-in-dressing-room-world-cup-2023-2023-11-21-903772, and https://www.livemint.com/sports/cricket-news/pakistans-cricket-legends-hail-indian-cricket-team-wasim-akram-calls-world-cup-final-one-bad-day-11700539252303.html etc., but nowhere there was a word about the whole World Cup having been totally fake. The dense world full of imbeciles (as we have seen) is always too keen to lap up irrelevant non-sense.

Just think of it; when there has not been any Cricket at all for past some decades, only a façade in its name, **doesn't anything said related to it anywhere or through any medium, assuming it to be a sport all these years, become all worthless bunkum?** And there have been hundreds of tonnes of it, especially in the Indian Media.

Similarly, there are volumes said and written about cricket statistics and the myriad records. And the intellectuals the world over continue to go gaga over these meaningless things whose origin lies in thoroughly fake Cricket. Questions are frequently asked in the famous and very popular Indian reality show '*Kaun Banega Crorepati?*' based on these statistics, the contestants expected to be fully knowledgeable about the developments over the years in the thoroughly fake sport. **How dense the human world can be! Continuing to inflict the biggest known and proven public fraud and crime on itself!**

Could anyone beat it? Someone, a great political leader at the world stage, who himself promotes/blesses a big source of terror funding (Cricket), saying such things time and again: https://www.indiatoday.in/india/video/we-can-never-forget-this-day-pm-modi-on-15-years-of-2611-mumbai-attacks-2467647-2023-11-26. And a whole country being similarly hypocritical: https://www.deccanherald.com/india/india-remembers-victims-of-2611-mumbai-attacks-leaders-reaffirm-pledge-to-fight-terrorism-2785720.

Let us see another totally hollow beating about the bush, another attempt only at politicization, another balderdash with no worthwhile substance, no botheration about what Cricket has been, a successfully marketed video (there were more than 10000 comments at the time of writing it, and millions of views) containing total trash from a thoroughly ignorant man who appears to know nothing about the reality of Cricket: https://m.youtube.com/watch?v=kLBD9uQK7JA. This video came to my notice at the very last moment of finalizing the draft of this book. No wonder, I felt all the more aghast at such worthless videos being lapped up by the masses, at another clear manifestation of the dense world around me.

The interview of Mr. Amit Majithia by a highly ignorant interviewer referred in the last chapter also is totally bunkum as far as fixing in Cricket is concerned. It amounts to sending the viewers on some wild goose chase. Mr. Majithia either is too ignorant a man or does not talk of the real thing – the institutional ball-by-ball fixing – on purpose. Such videos aplenty doing the rounds even today after the reality lies repeatedly exposed in the public domain for last ten years, duly confirmed by a key insider Sanjeev Chawla more than 2 years ago, further establish the extreme denseness of the present day world.

I have said enough under the chapter '**The Criminal Media**' in my last book as to how fake Cricket is promoted and marketed by the rogue media through its daily Headlines. Same was all the more on show during this World Cup; more towards the end and especially in India. The front page headlines of various national dailies discussed Cricket as a sport, deliberating a lot on the fake

World Cup matches, like https://www.thestatesman.com/sports/india-look-to-avenge-2019-semifinal-heartbreak-against-new-zealand-1503240759.html. The Media, having full knowledge of the reality, never even remotely let people know how fake Cricket was that it had so keenly been marketing for decades. The world remaining as dense and as stupid as it was suited the media's villainous existence.

Probably the denseness of the world or the collective human stupidity got culminated in the behaviour of the all-powerful Supreme Court of India. Inaction by it since 2018 (after filing of a writ petition before it on the subject in November, 2017), despite an encyclopaedia of evidence presented to it of the ongoing colossal public fraud, of the elephantine wrong-doings (even by a multitude of authorities including the judicial ones), has ensured that the recently concluded ICC Men's CWC 2023 was as fake as Cricket around the globe has been for past some decades.

❑❑❑

About the Author

Atul Kumar is an engineer, a postgraduate from IIT Madras. He served the Indian Railways as a Class I officer from 1981 to 2011 before taking voluntary retirement. While in service, he was instrumental in exposing leakage of approximately Rs 5000 crores per year through cartels in Railway procurement. As a consequence, he was awarded S R Jindal Prize 2011 for crusade against corruption at the national level.

Atul Kumar is also an awarded poet in Hindi. Many of his poetry books have been published.

Around 2013, after retirement, Atul Kumar exposed the ball-by-ball institutionalised fixing in Cricket through his books and press conferences etc. Some background details are available on the website: **thecricketmafia.com.**

Atul Kumar also wrote a book on the genocide through Covid in English. The same has been translated in Hindi also. Whatever he said about the ongoing catastrophe then, from application of common-sense, stands fully validated today. In this book, he has propounded a pertinent law, ***'Law of Collective Stupidity'***.

Most of the books written by him can be seen through this link: https://www.amazon.in/kindle-dbs/entity/author/B0BKFSBLDV?_encoding=UTF8&node=976389031&offset=0&pageSize=12&searchAlias=stripbooks&sort=author-sidecar-rank&page=1&langFilter=default#formatSelectorHeader.

Many of these books, including the poetry ones, have no parallel.

Email: atulrailway@hotmail.com;

***